RAND McNALLY



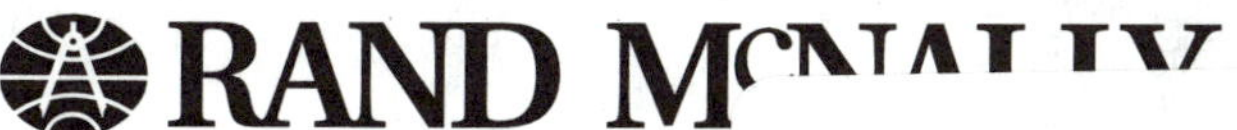

# Kids' Road Atlas

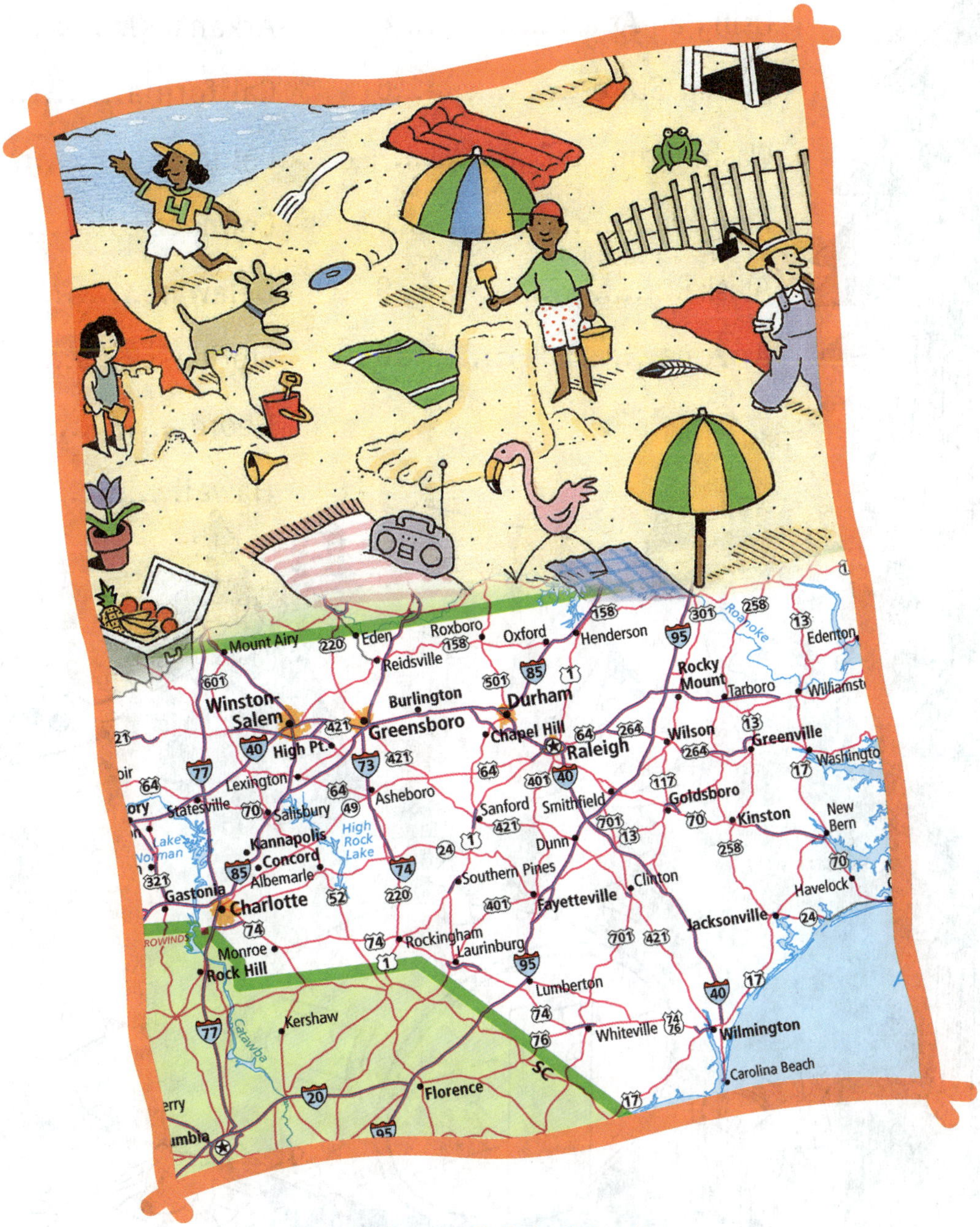


Rand McNally for Kids™

# Table of Contents

# Using an Atlas...

## Adventure or Mystery?

Is map reading an adventure or a mystery? It's only a mystery if you haven't uncovered the clues and codes. The information below will help you unlock the mystery and get started on the adventure. Solve the clues and use the numbered letters to fill in the secret message. For some of the clues you'll need to use the legend, scale, and coordinates, but for others you'll have to do a bit more detective work. Take a closer look at the maps for familiar cities, bordering states, and other details to help you find the answers. Good luck!

**Legend**

| | | |
|---|---|---|
| Interstate Highways 65 | Free Limited Access | Rivers/Canals |
| U.S. Highways 82 | Toll Limited Access Highways | Lakes/Reservoir |
| State and Provincial Highways 5 | Principal Through Highways | National Monument |
| Canadian Shield 16 | Other Highways | Park Areas |
| Mexican Shield 49 | | City Areas |
| Cities & Towns | | |
| Capitals | | |

## LEGEND

The legend, or map key, is a description of the symbols and lines on the map. Use the legend at the left for all of the maps in *Kids' Road Atlas*.

**Clue # 1:** What National Park is at the southernmost section of the map at the right?

___ ___ ___ ___ ___ ___ ___ ___ ___ ___ National Park

(blank 5 = 1, blank 10 = 2)

**Clue # 2:** In what state will you find this park?

___ ___ ___ ___ ___ ___ ___

(blank 5 = 3, blank 6 = 4)

## SCALE

Maps come in all sizes; some show the whole world and others show only a small neighborhood. The map scale tells you how space on a map equals distance on the earth. Scale is used to measure distances between places on a map. Measure the length of the distance from place to place on the map and then use the scale to find out how many miles or kilometers that is. The maps in *Kids' Road Atlas* are not all at the same scale, so be sure to look at the scale on each map to measure distance correctly.

**Clue # 3:** On the map at the right, what "mile-high" city is approximately 30 miles southeast of Boulder on Interstate 70?

___ ___ ___ ___ ___ ___

5 6

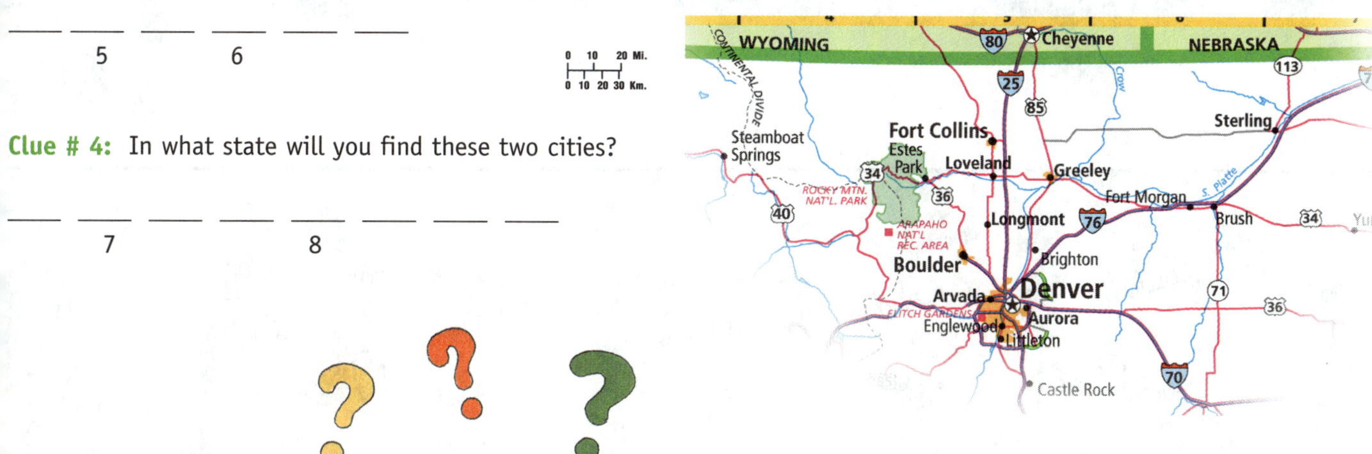


**Clue # 4:** In what state will you find these two cities?

___ ___ ___ ___ ___ ___ ___ ___

7 8

## COORDINATES

A coordinate is a letter-number combination that helps you find places on a map. To locate a city, look in the index to find the coordinate for that city. If, for example, the coordinate for the city is B-5, look down the right or left edge of the map for the letter B and draw an imaginary line across the map. Then, look across the top or bottom of the map for the number 5 and draw an imaginary line down or up until it crosses the imaginary line drawn from the letter B. The city will be inside the area around this point. For each map in the *Kids' Road Atlas* there is a yellow coordinate border with letters and numbers.

**Clue # 5:** What coastal city on the map below is at coordinate I-6? Hint: There are several, so make sure you pick the one that fits in the blanks.

___ ___ ___ ___ ___ ___ ___   ___ ___ ___ ___ ___

9 10 11 12

**Clue # 6:** In what state is this city?

___ ___ ___ ___ ___ ___ ___ ___ ___ ___

13 14

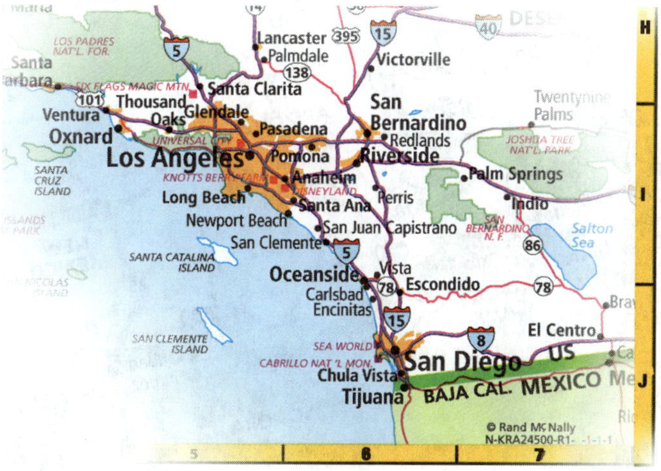

**Clue # 7:** You'll find this Mexican city at coordinate J-6.

___ ___ ___ ___ ___ ___ ___

15 16 17

**Secret Message:**

___ ___ ___   ___ ___ ___ ___ ___ ___ ___ ___ ___

15 12 5   17 4 6 5 14 15 16 8 5

___ ___ ___ ___ ___ ___   ___ ___ ___ ___   ___   ___ ___ ___ ___

11 5 1 3 14 2   9 3 15 12   17   15 16 8 14

___ ___   ___ ___ ___   ___ ___ ___ ___!

7 13   15 12 5   10 17 1 5

# United States

Capital:
Washington, D.C.

CANADA
BRITISH COLUMBIA
ALBERTA
SASKATCHEWAN
MANITOBA
ONTARIO
Tatla Lake
Edmonton
Kamloops
Vancouver
Calgary
Lethbridge
Regina
Winnipeg
Lake Winnipeg
Thunder Bay
Lake Superior

WASHINGTON
OREGON
IDAHO
MONTANA
WYOMING
NORTH DAKOTA
SOUTH DAKOTA
MINNESOTA
WISCONSIN
MICHIGAN
IOWA
NEBRASKA
NEVADA
UTAH
COLORADO
CALIFORNIA
KANSAS
ILLINOIS
IND
KENTU
MISSOURI
OKLAHOMA
ARKANSAS
TENN
ARIZONA
NEW MEXICO
TEXAS
LOUISIANA
MISSISSIPPI
ALABA

Olympia
Seattle
Spokane
Portland
Salem
Boise
Missoula
Great Falls
Helena
Butte
Billings
Idaho Falls
Pocatello
Casper
Rapid City
Bismarck
Fargo
Duluth
St. Paul
Minneapolis
Sioux Falls
Green Bay
Madison
Milwaukee
Muskegon
Lansing
L. Michigan
Great Salt Lake
Salt Lake City
Reno
Sacramento
San Francisco
Oakland
Cheyenne
Denver
Colorado Springs
Pueblo
Omaha
Lincoln
Des Moines
Davenport
Chicago
Quincy
Springfield
Indianapolis
Topeka
Kansas City
St. Louis
Louisville
Wichita
Springfield
Nashville
Las Vegas
Los Angeles
San Diego
Santa Fe
Albuquerque
Amarillo
Oklahoma City
Tulsa
Memphis
Little Rock
Birmingham
Phoenix
Tucson
El Paso
Lubbock
Abilene
Ft. Worth
Dallas
Shreveport
Jackson
Montgomery
Alexandria
Austin
Beaumont
Baton Rouge
Mobile
New Orleans
Houston
Galveston
San Antonio
Laredo
Corpus Christi

MEXICO
BAJA CALIF.
BAJA CALIF. SUR
SONORA
CHIHUAHUA
COAHUILA
SINALOA
DURANGO
NUEVO LEON
ZACATECAS
SAN LUIS POTOSI
TAMAULIPAS
Ensenada
Mexicali
Nogales
Ciudad Juárez
Hermosillo
Santa Rosalía
Ciudad Obregón
Los Mochis
La Paz
Gómez Palacio
Nuevo Laredo
Monterrey
Reynosa
Mazatlán
Zacatecas

PACIFIC OCEAN
GULF OF MEXICO

5 82 90 84 15 94 29 35 86 80 25 76 70 135 335 44 40 405 10 17 8 19 27 20 30 49 45 37 55 59 12 24 65 64 57 72 74 39 43 69

0 100 200
0 100 200 300

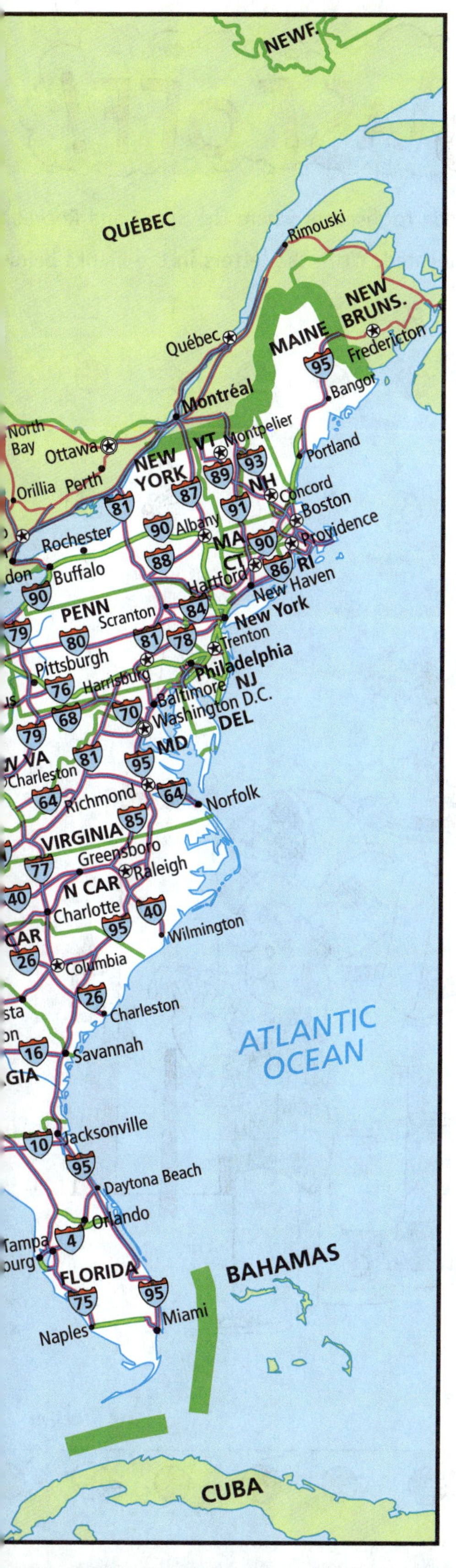

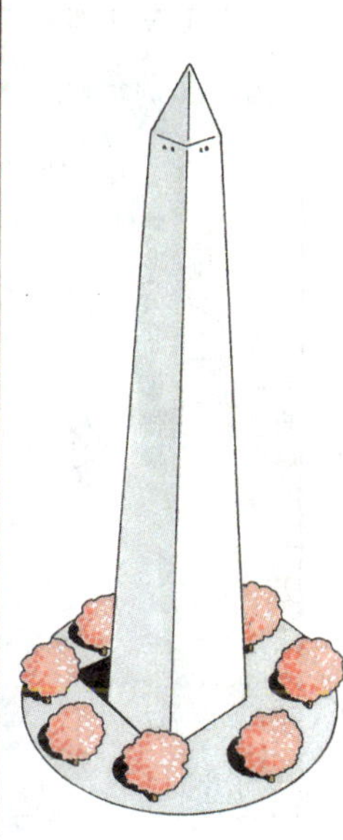

# KEEP IT BRIEF

Each state has a two-letter abbreviation. Write the abbreviation for each state name in the blanks below. Remember that the two-letter abbreviation should be written in capital letters. Hint: Check out the state names in the blue bar at the top of the pages in the book. The two letters of the abbreviation are the two capital letters in the name.

1. Alabama ______
2. Alaska ______
3. Arizona ______
4. Arkansas ______
5. California ______
6. Colorado ______
7. Connecticut ______
8. Delaware ______
9. Florida ______
10. Georgia ______
11. Hawaii ______
12. Idaho ______
13. Illinois ______
14. Indiana ______
15. Iowa ______
16. Kansas ______
17. Kentucky ______
18. Louisiana ______
19. Maine ______
20. Maryland ______
21. Massachusetts ______
22. Michigan ______
23. Minnesota ______
24. Mississippi ______
25. Missouri ______
26. Montana ______
27. Nebraska ______
28. Nevada ______
29. New Hampshire ______
30. New Jersey ______
31. New Mexico ______
32. New York ______
33. North Carolina ______
34. North Dakota ______
35. Ohio ______
36. Oklahoma ______
37. Oregon ______
38. Pennsylvania ______
39. Rhode Island ______
40. South Carolina ______
41. South Dakota ______
42. Tennessee ______
43. Texas ______
44. Utah ______
45. Vermont ______
46. Virginia ______
47. Washington ______
48. West Virginia ______
49. Wisconsin ______
50. Wyoming ______

# Alabama

Heart of Dixie

Capital: Montgomery

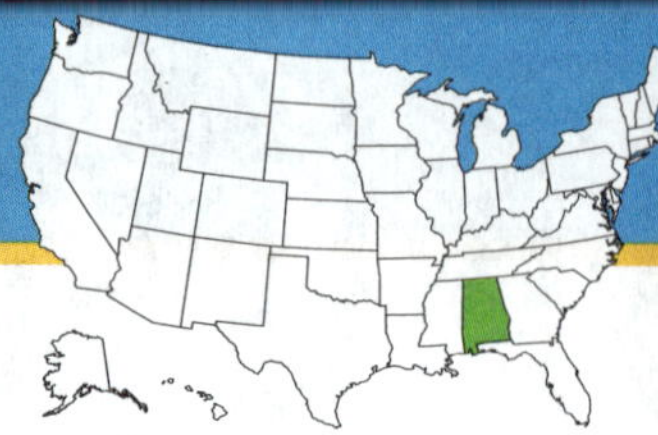

Southern Pine

Camellia

Yellowhammer

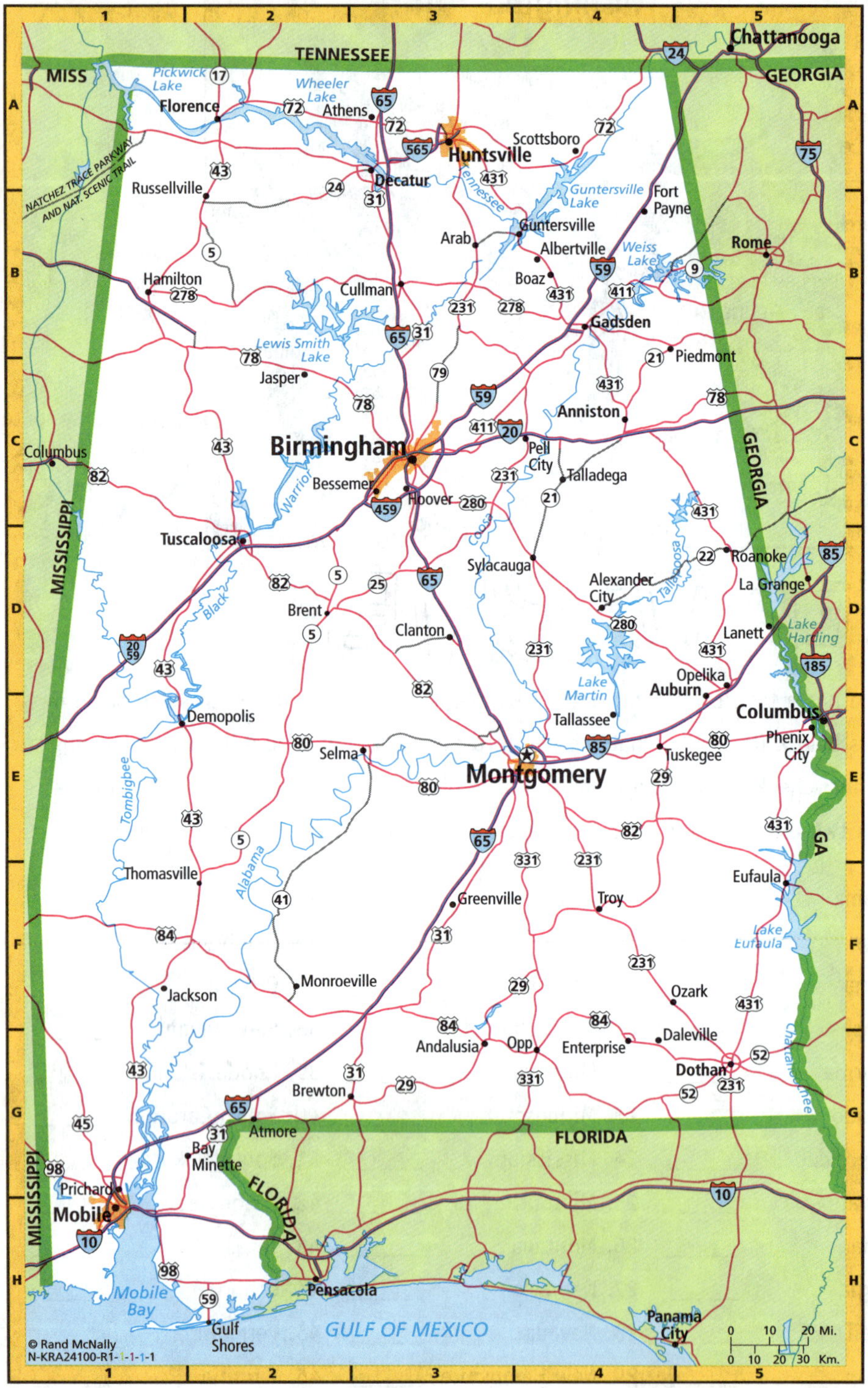

TENNESSEE
MISS
GEORGIA
Chattanooga
Pickwick Lake
Wheeler Lake
Florence
Athens
Huntsville
Scottsboro
Decatur
Russellville
NATCHEZ TRACE PARKWAY AND NAT. SCENIC TRAIL
Guntersville Lake
Fort Payne
Guntersville
Arab
Albertville
Weiss Lake
Rome
Hamilton
Cullman
Boaz
Gadsden
Lewis Smith Lake
Jasper
Piedmont
Anniston
Columbus
Birmingham
Pell City
Talladega
Bessemer
Hoover
Warrior
Tuscaloosa
Sylacauga
Roanoke
La Grange
Alexander City
Brent
Clanton
Lanett
Lake Harding
Black
Lake Martin
Opelika
Auburn
Columbus
Demopolis
Tallassee
Phenix City
Selma
Montgomery
Tuskegee
Tombigbee
Alabama
Thomasville
Greenville
Troy
Eufaula
Lake Eufaula
Monroeville
Jackson
Ozark
Andalusia
Opp
Enterprise
Daleville
Dothan
Chattahoochee
Brewton
Atmore
FLORIDA
Bay Minette
Prichard
Mobile
Mobile Bay
Pensacola
Gulf Shores
GULF OF MEXICO
Panama City
MISSISSIPPI
GEORGIA
GA
0 10 20 Mi.
0 10 20 30 Km.

Use the code to discover where the Space and Rocket Center is located. Write the letters in the blanks below.

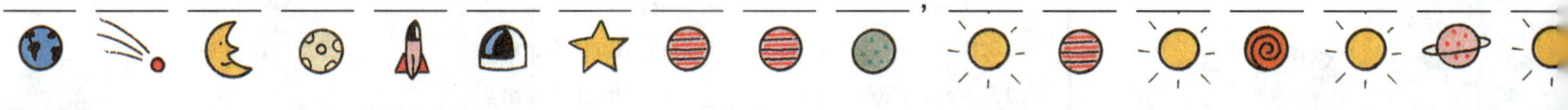

___ ___ ___ ___ ___ ___ ___ ___ ___ ___ , ___ ___ ___ ___ ___ ___ ___

        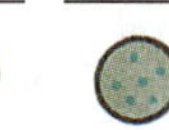        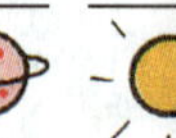

# Alaska

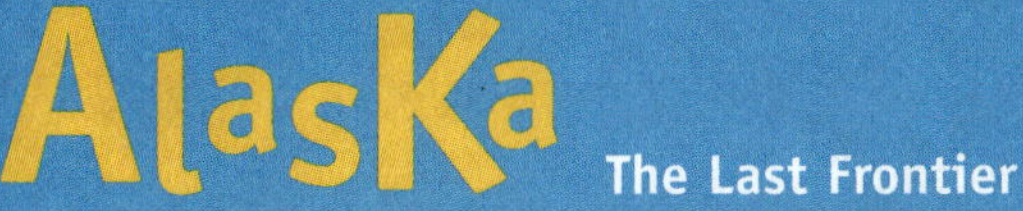

The Last Frontier

Capital:
Juneau

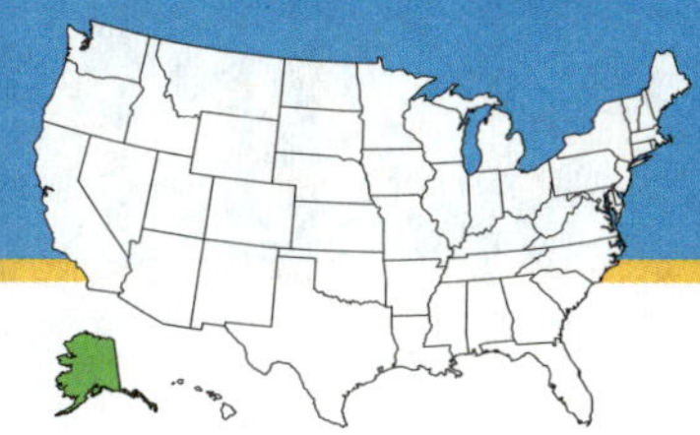

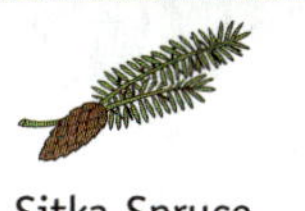

Sitka Spruce

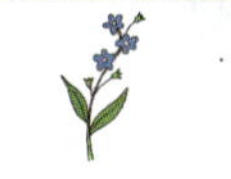

Forget-me-not

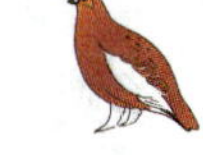

Willow Ptarmigan

## DISCOVERING ALASKA

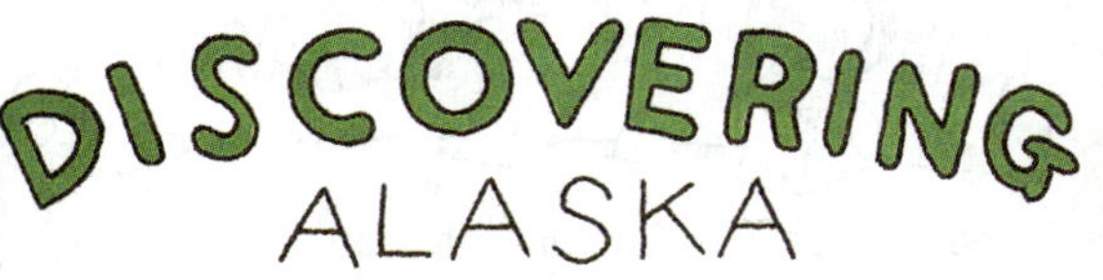

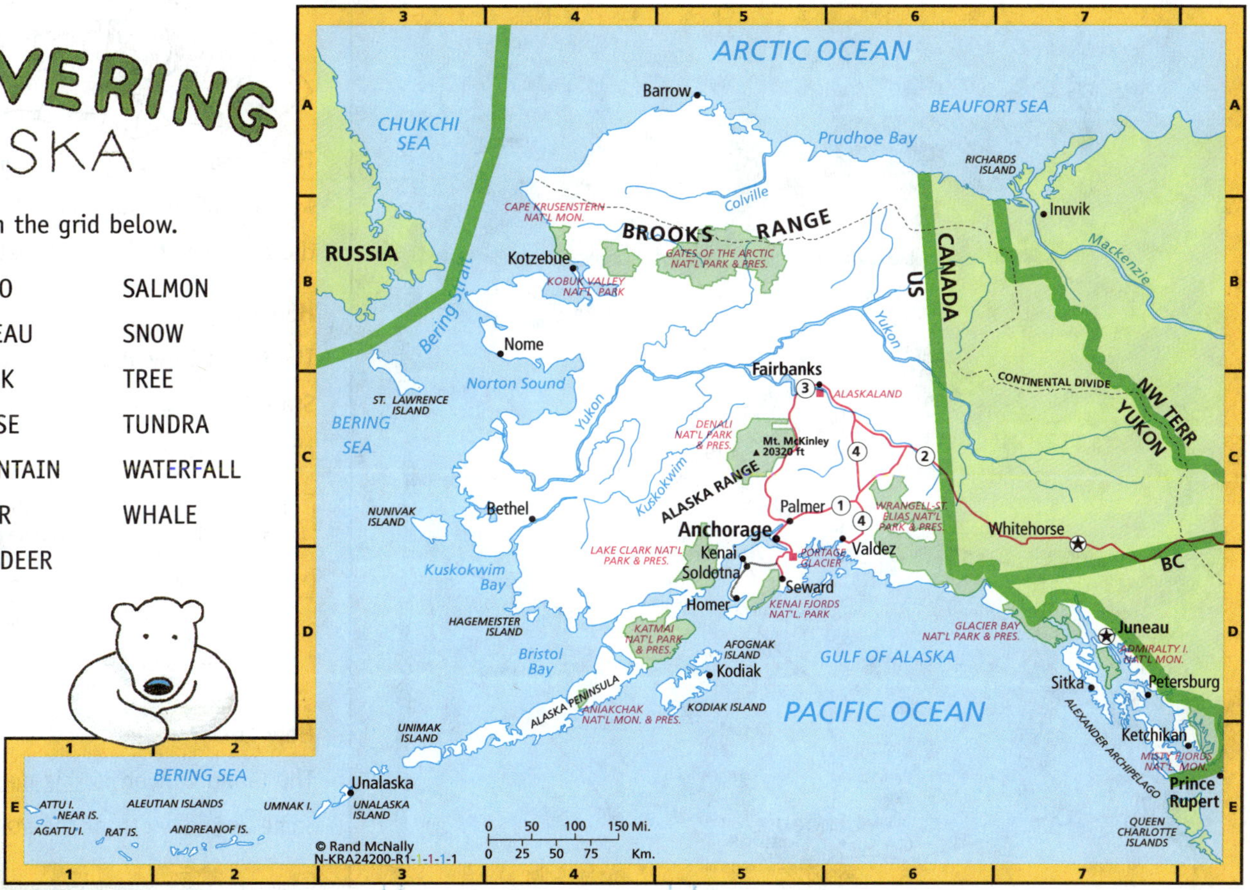

Circle the Alaska words in the grid below.

| | | |
|---|---|---|
| ANCHORAGE | IGLOO | SALMON |
| BALD EAGLE | JUNEAU | SNOW |
| DOG SLED RACE | KAYAK | TREE |
| ESKIMO | MOOSE | TUNDRA |
| GLACIER | MOUNTAIN | WATERFALL |
| GOLD | OTTER | WHALE |
| GRIZZLY BEAR | REINDEER | |

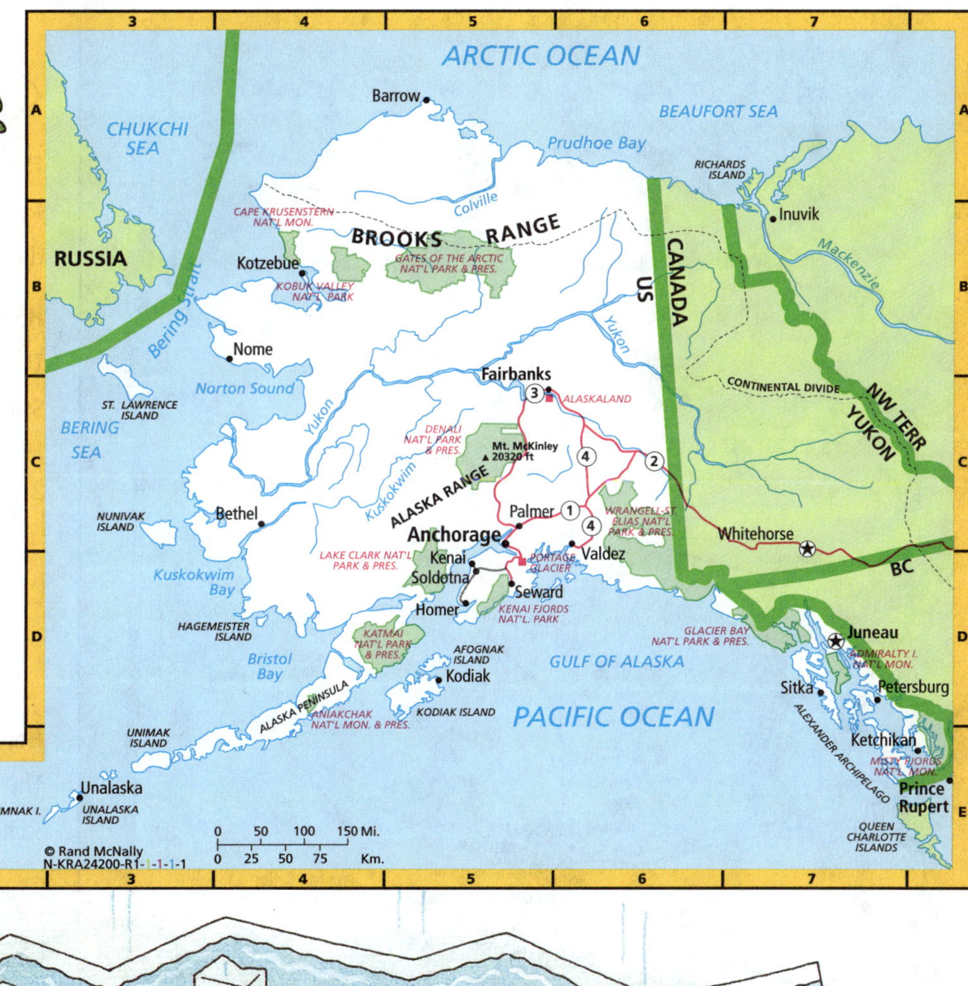

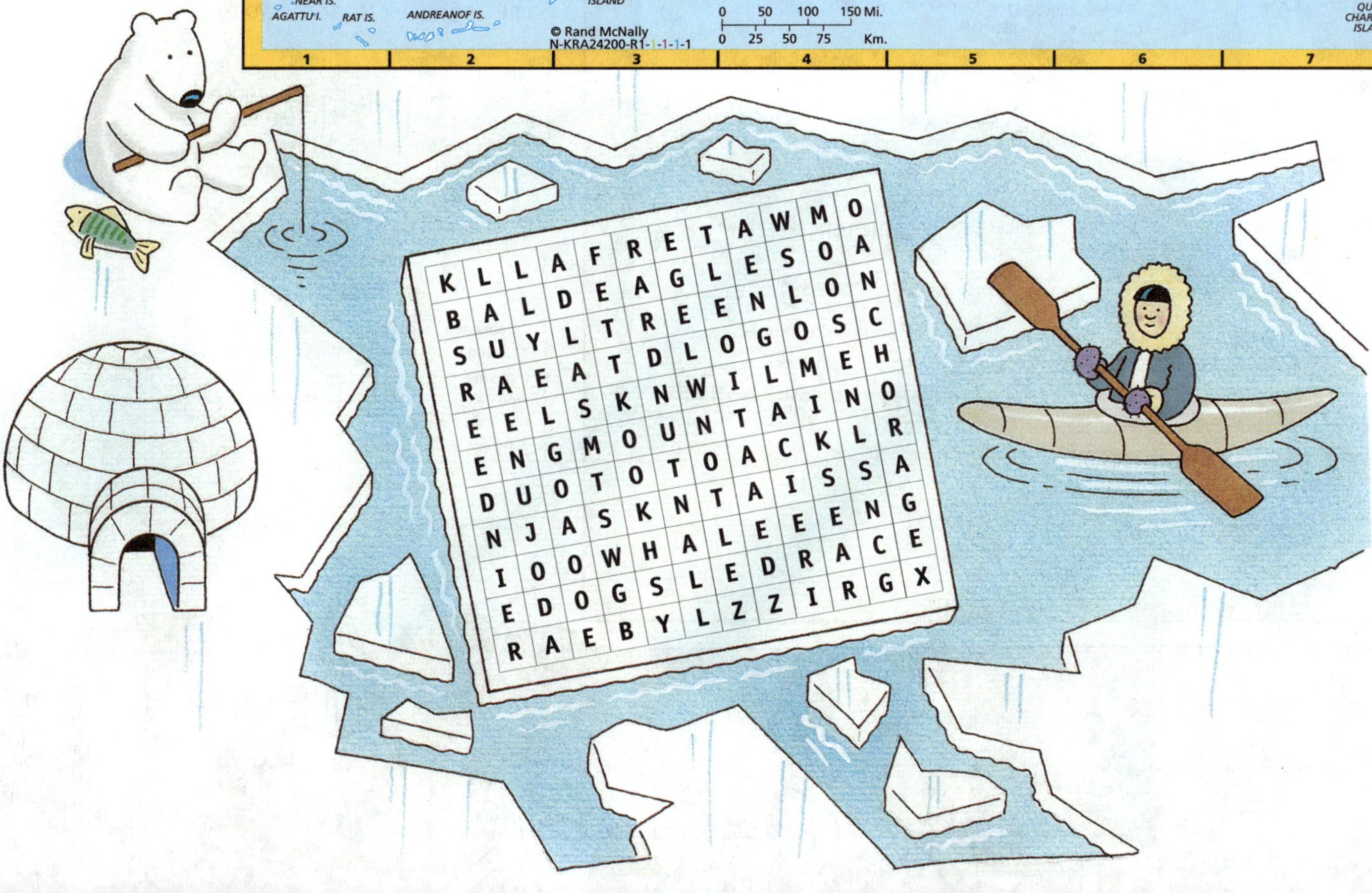

| | | | | | | | | | | | |
|---|---|---|---|---|---|---|---|---|---|---|---|
| K | L | L | A | F | R | E | T | A | W | M | O |
| B | A | L | D | E | A | G | L | E | S | O | A |
| S | U | Y | L | T | R | E | E | N | L | O | N |
| R | A | E | A | T | D | L | O | G | O | S | C |
| E | E | L | S | K | N | W | I | L | M | E | H |
| E | N | G | M | O | U | N | T | A | I | N | O |
| D | U | O | T | O | T | O | A | C | K | L | R |
| N | J | A | S | K | N | T | A | I | S | S | A |
| I | O | O | W | H | A | L | E | E | E | N | G |
| E | D | O | G | S | L | E | D | R | A | C | E |
| R | A | E | B | Y | L | Z | Z | I | R | G | X |

# ArIZona

Grand Canyon State

Capital: Phoenix

Palo Verde    Saguaro Cactus Blossom    Cactus Wren

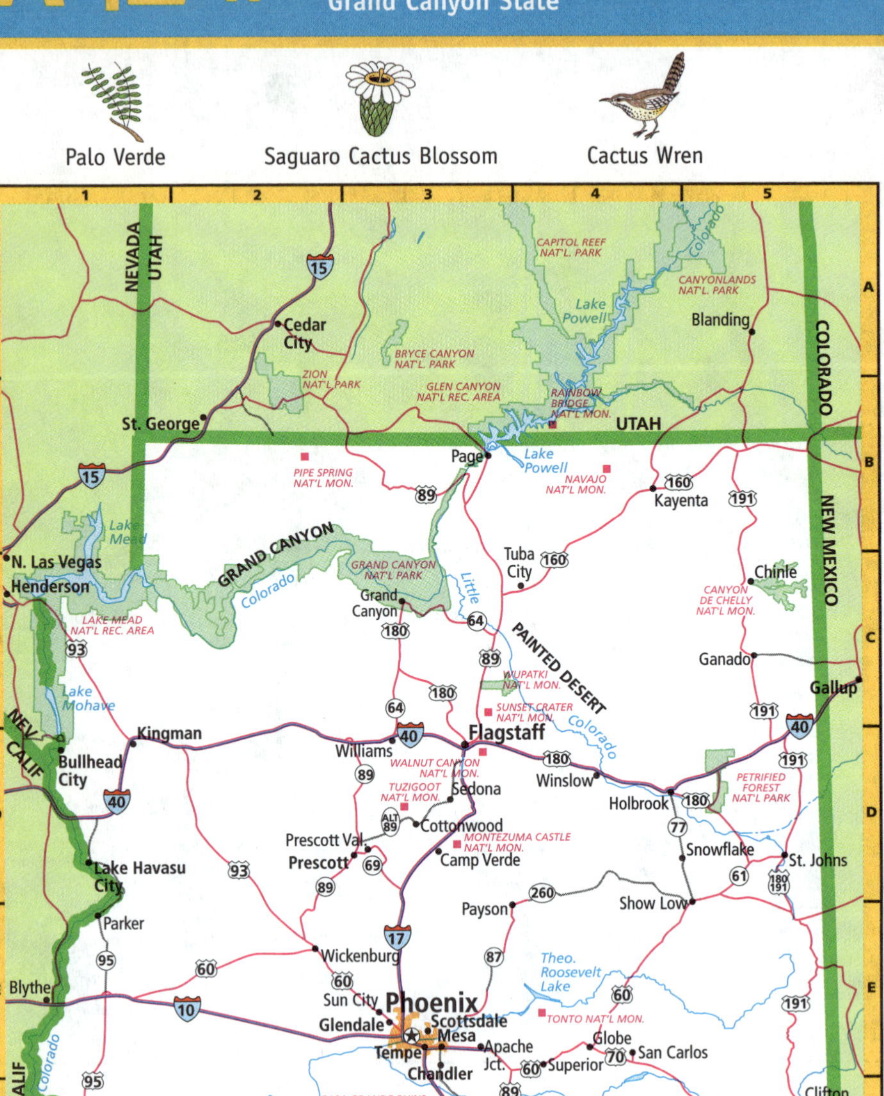

The Grand Canyon (C-2) is one of the seven natural wonders of the world and its size is incredible. Solve the problems to find out just how big it is.

### How Deep?

The Grand Canyon could fit this many Empire State Buildings inside its walls, stacked on top of one another!

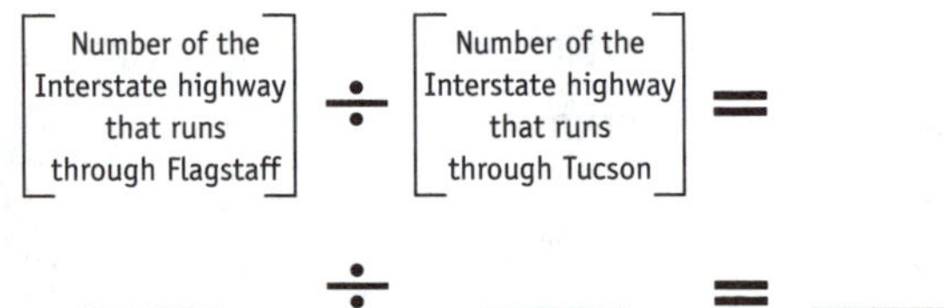


_____ ÷ _____ = _____

### How Long?

The Grand Canyon is this many miles long, almost the same as the width of the state of Illinois!

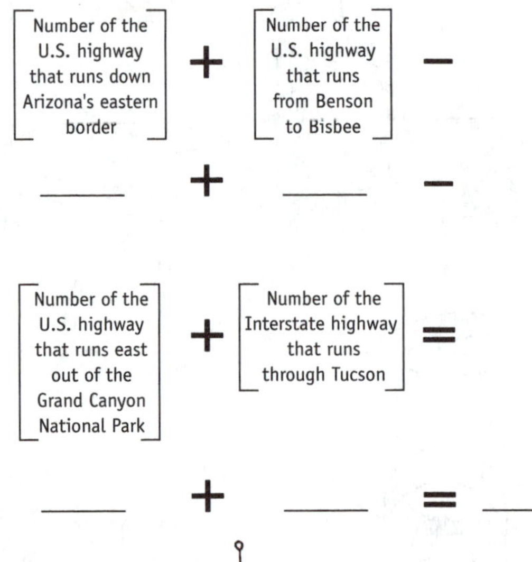

# ARkansas

The Natural State

Capital:
Little Rock

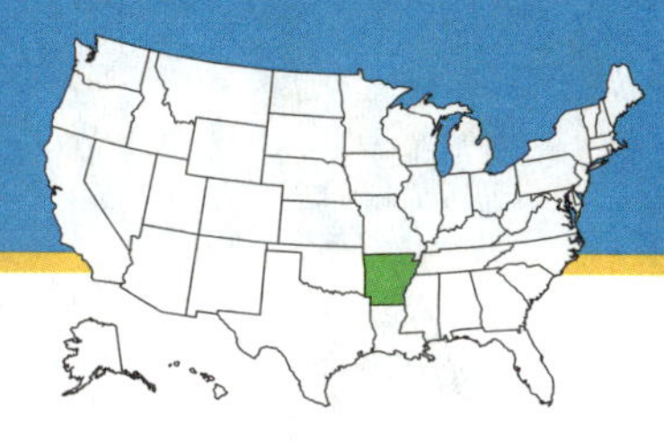

Pine

Apple Blossom

Mockingbird

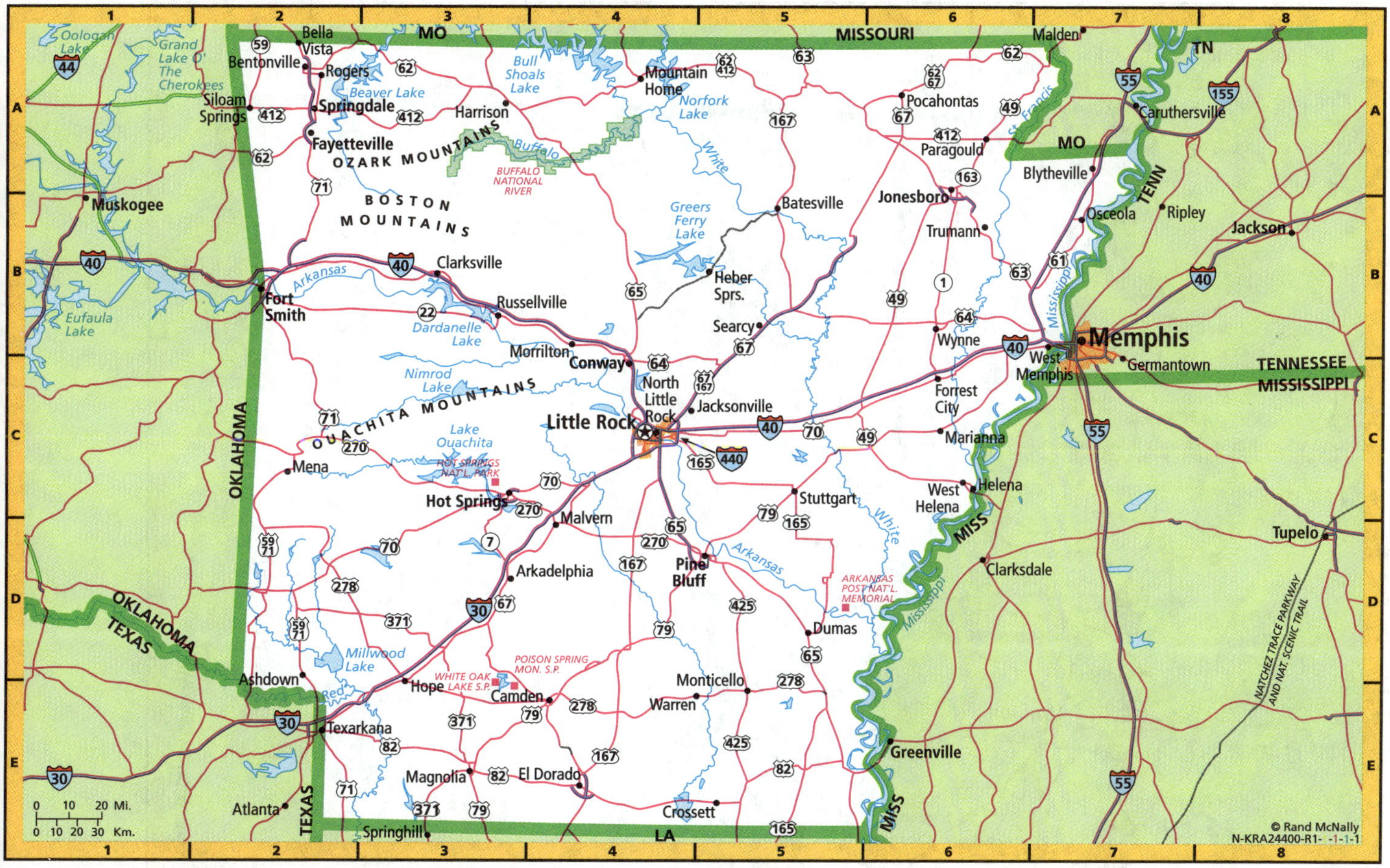

## ROAD RALLY

It's a road rally from Dumas (D–5) to where? When you race in a rally you are given a map with your beginning city only. Can you figure out which towns are on the route after Dumas to the finish?

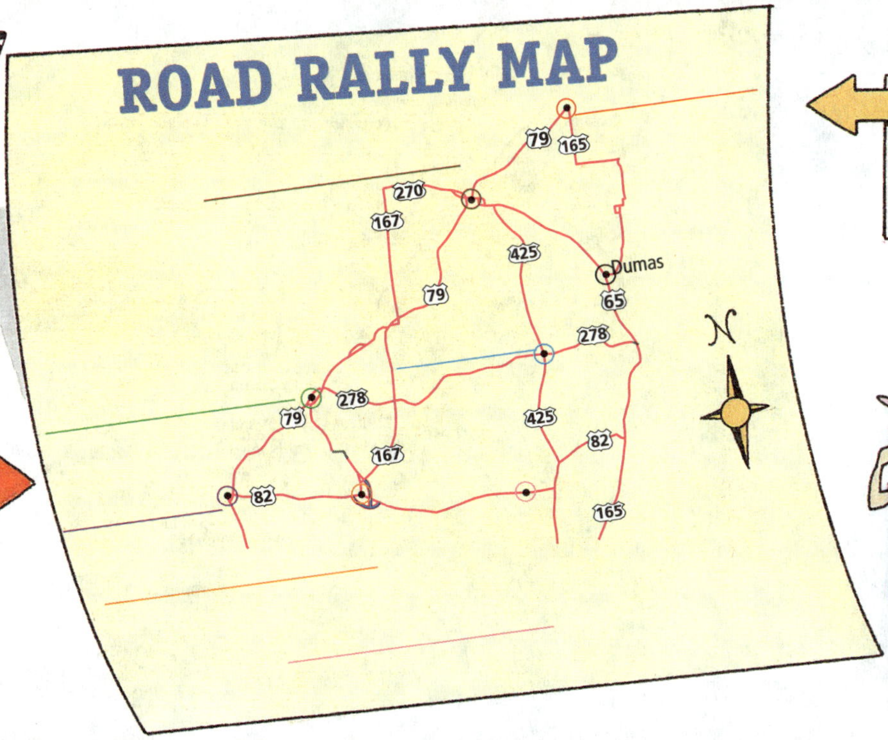

ROAD RALLY MAP

# California

The Golden State

Capital: Sacramento

California Redwood

Golden Poppy

California Valley Quail

Grants Pass
Medford
Ashland
Klamath Falls
OREG
OREG
NEV
IDAHO
NEV
Goose Lake
MODOC NAT'L. FOR.
LAVA BEDS NAT'L. MON.
KLAMATH NATIONAL FOREST
Yreka
COAST RANGES
REDWOOD NAT'L. PK.
SIX RIVERS NAT'L FOREST
Arcata
Eureka
WHISKEYTOWN SHASTA-TRINITY NAT'L REC. AREA
Lake Shasta
Redding
LASSEN VOLCANIC NAT'L. PK.
Susanville
TRINITY NATIONAL FOREST
Red Bluff
Sacramento
Corning
Orland
Paradise
Chico
Oroville
Willows
Fort Bragg
Willits
Ukiah
Yuba City
Marysville
Winnemucca
Elko
UTAH
NEV
Pyramid Lake
Sparks
Reno
Carson City
Lake Tahoe
Auburn
Roseville
S. Lake Tahoe
Ely
Walker Lake
Hawthorne
GREAT BASIN NAT'L. PARK
Healdsburg
Woodland
Placerville
Santa Rosa
Sacramento
SIERRA NEVADA
Napa
Fairfield
Vallejo
Lodi
POINT REYES NAT'L SEASHORE
Novato
Berkeley
Stockton
MUIR WOODS NAT'L MON.
Oakland
Manteca
YOSEMITE NATIONAL PARK
Mono Lake
San Francisco
Modesto
DEVILS POSTPILE NAT'L MON.
Fremont
Turlock
San Joaquin
Palo Alto
PARAMOUNT'S GREAT AMERICA
Merced
San Jose
SIERRA NAT'L FOREST
Los Banos
Chowchilla
Madera
KINGS CANYON N. P.
Santa Cruz
Gilroy
Watsonville
Hollister
Monterey Bay
Clovis
Monterey
Salinas
Fresno
Selma
PINNACLES NAT'L MON.
SEQUOIA N. P.
DEATH VALLEY NATIONAL PARK
DEVIL'S HOLE (DEATH VALLEY) NAT'L PARK
Soledad
Hanford
Visalia
Lemoore
Tulare
Lindsay
Porterville
King City
Coalinga
Las Vegas
N. Las Vegas
Henderson
Lake Mead
Boulder City
LAKE MEAD NAT'L. REC. AREA
Delano
Paso Robles
Wasco
McFarland
Ridgecrest
Cambria
Atascadero
Morro Bay
Bakersfield
San Luis Obispo
Arroyo Grande
Taft
Tehachapi
MOJAVE DESERT
Barstow
Santa Maria
Needles
LOS PADRES NAT'L. FOR.
Lancaster
Palmdale
Victorville
Lompoc
Santa Barbara
SIX FLAGS MAGIC MTN.
Santa Clarita
Twentynine Palms
Ventura
Thousand Oaks
Glendale
San Bernardino
Oxnard
Pasadena
Redlands
UNIVERSAL CITY
JOSHUA TREE NAT'L. PARK
PACIFIC OCEAN
SAN MIGUEL ISLAND
Los Angeles
Pomona
Riverside
ARIZ
SANTA ROSA ISLAND
SANTA CRUZ ISLAND
KNOTTS BERRY FARM
Anaheim
DISNEYLAND
Palm Springs
Long Beach
Perris
Indio
Blythe
Santa Ana
Newport Beach
San Juan Capistrano
CHANNEL ISLANDS NATIONAL PARK
SAN BERNARDINO N. F.
Salton Sea
San Clemente
Colorado
SANTA CATALINA ISLAND
Oceanside
Vista
Escondido
SAN NICOLAS ISLAND
Carlsbad
Encinitas
Brawley
El Centro
Yuma
SAN CLEMENTE ISLAND
SEA WORLD
CABRILLO NAT'L MON.
San Diego
US
Calexico
Chula Vista
Tijuana
BAJA CAL.
MEXICO
Mexicali
San Luis Rio Colorado
SONORA
0 10 20 30 Mi.
0 10 20 30 40 Km.

# PARK IT HERE

Look on the map of California for the National Parks that are located at the coordinates listed below.

Write the names of the parks in the puzzle. The shaded column will spell out California's state motto, reading from top to bottom.

1. A–1
2. F–5
3. I–7
4. E–4
5. F–5
6. F–6

# Colorado

Centennial State

Capital: Denver

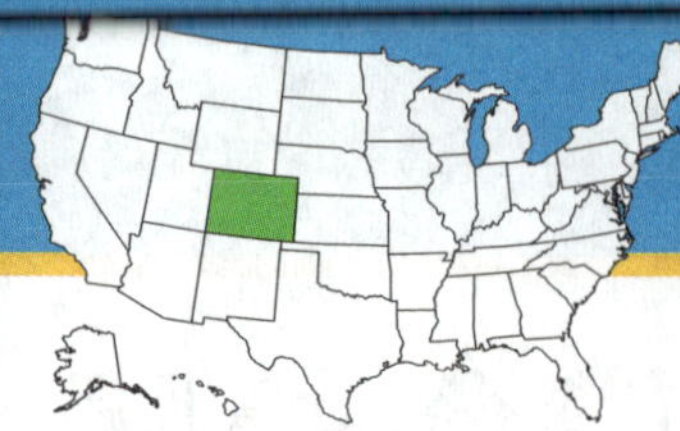

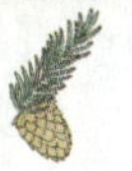

Colorado Blue Spruce

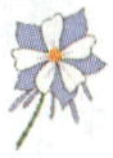

Columbine

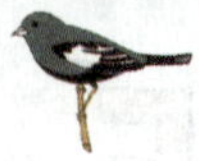

Lark Bunting

## THE NAME GAME

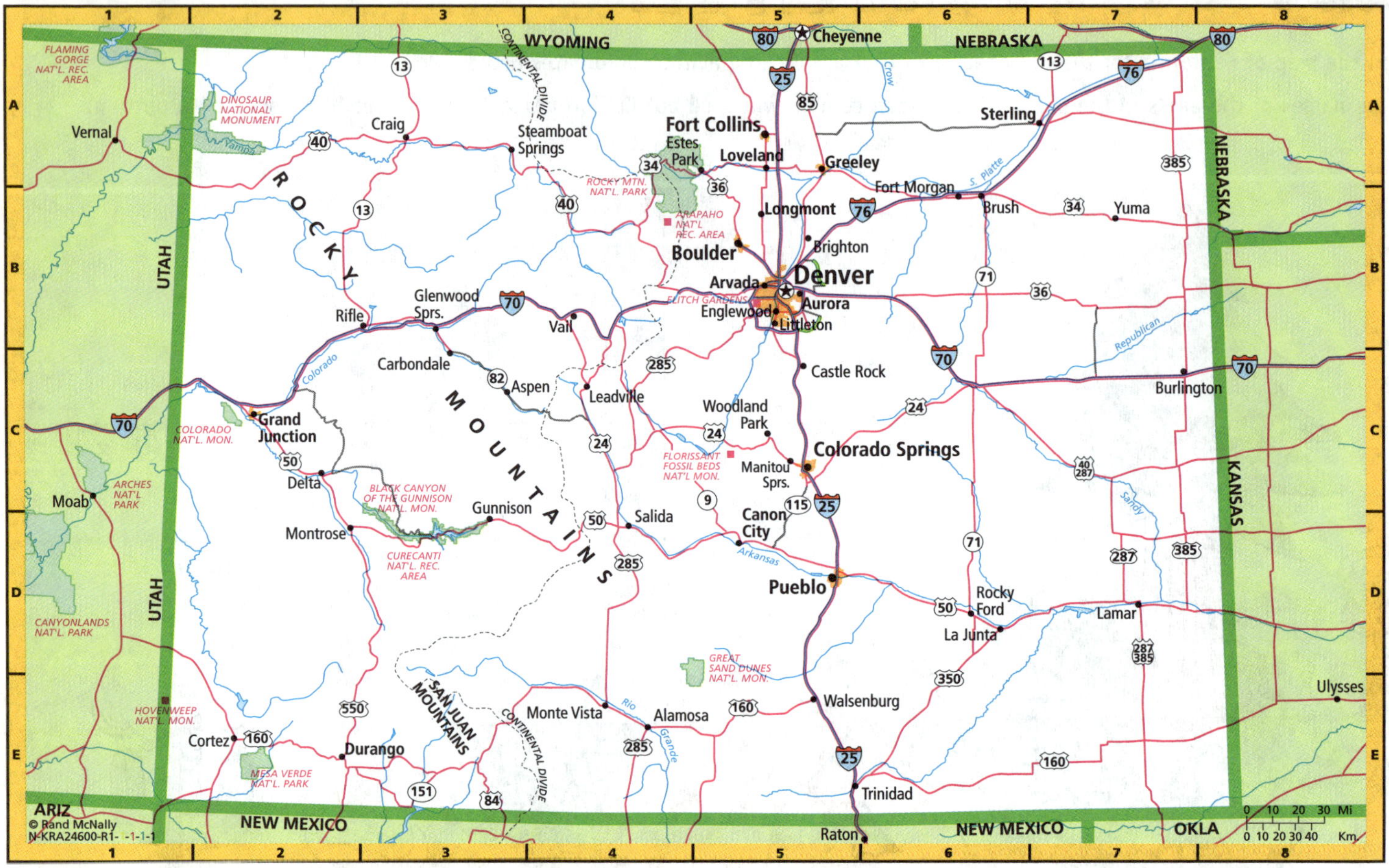

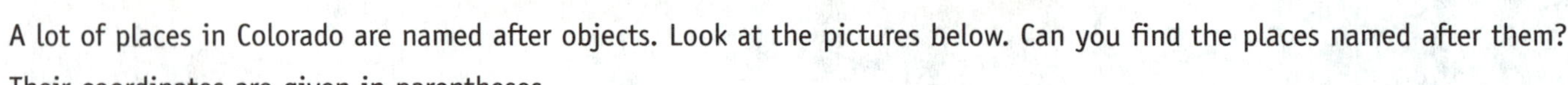

A lot of places in Colorado are named after objects. Look at the pictures below. Can you find the places named after them? Their coordinates are given in parentheses.

(C–3)

(B–5)

(B–3)

(A–3)

(River)

(A–6)

(B–6)

(A–2)

(C–5)

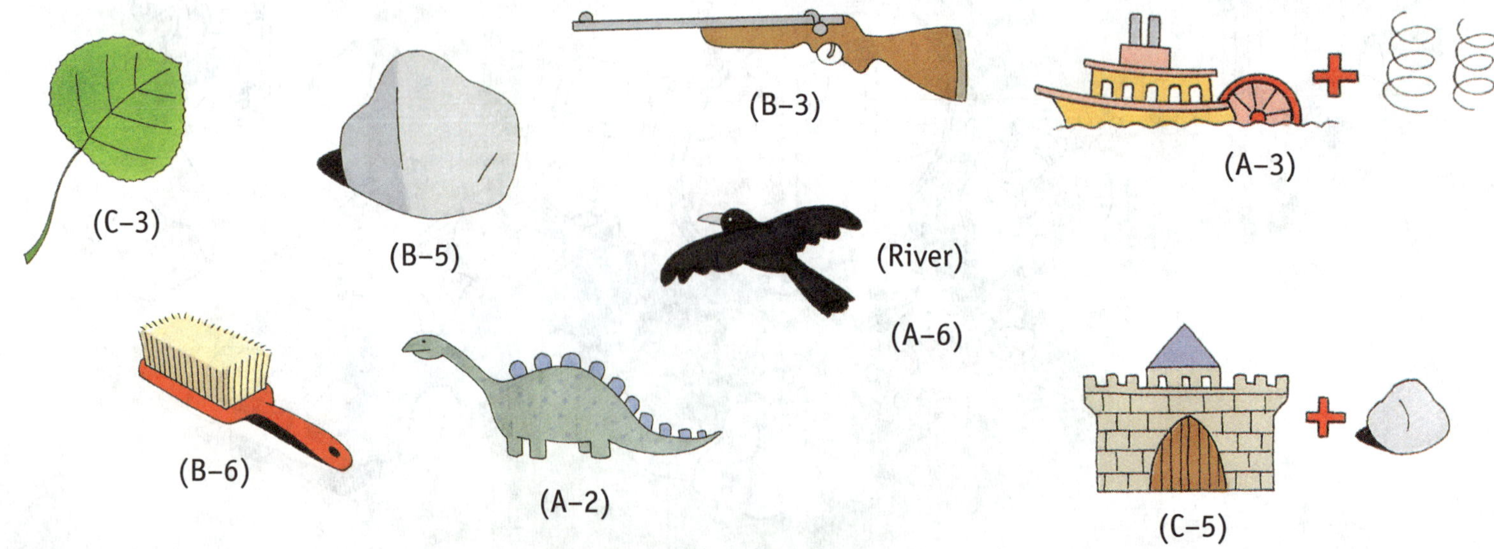

# Connecticut

Constitution State

Capital: Hartford

White Oak

Mountain Laurel

American Robin

Color the shapes that contain vowels to find out what's at the Mystic (C-5) Marinelife Aquarium.

Capital:
Dover

American Holly

Peach Blossom

Blue Hen Chicken

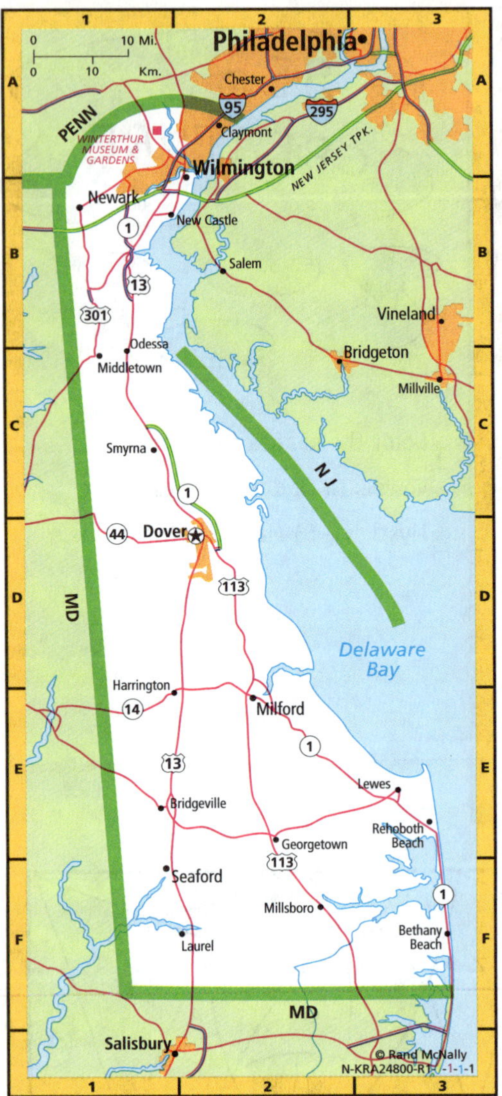

Delaware is well-known for its maritime history. Can you spot the correct reflection for this ship?

# Florida

Sunshine State

Capital: Tallahassee

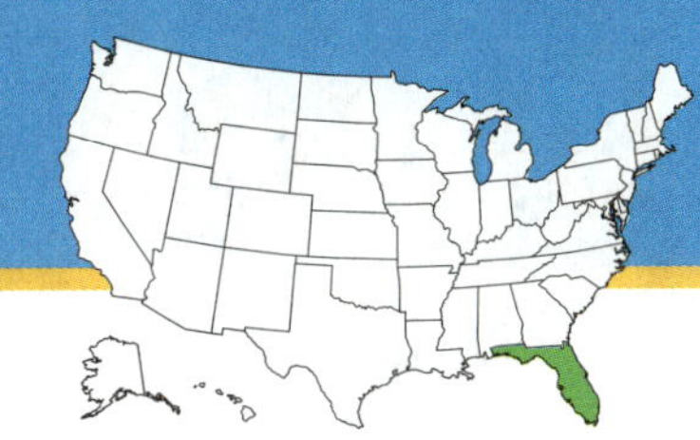

Sabal Palm

Orange Blossom

Mockingbird

The Florida beach below shows objects that can be grouped into pairs in which the letters of one thing can be rearranged to spell another. For example, HORSE and SHORE are a pair because they contain the same letters. Rearrange the letters in the words given to make other pairs.

| | | | |
|---|---|---|---|
| HORSE | SHORE | MELON | |
| OCEAN | | TEN | |
| PALM | | SHOE | |
| PEARS | | BEARD | |

# GeorgiA

Empire State of the South

Capital: Atlanta

Live Oak

Cherokee Rose

Brown Thrasher

Peanuts are an important crop in Georgia. Can you find your way through the peanut maze?

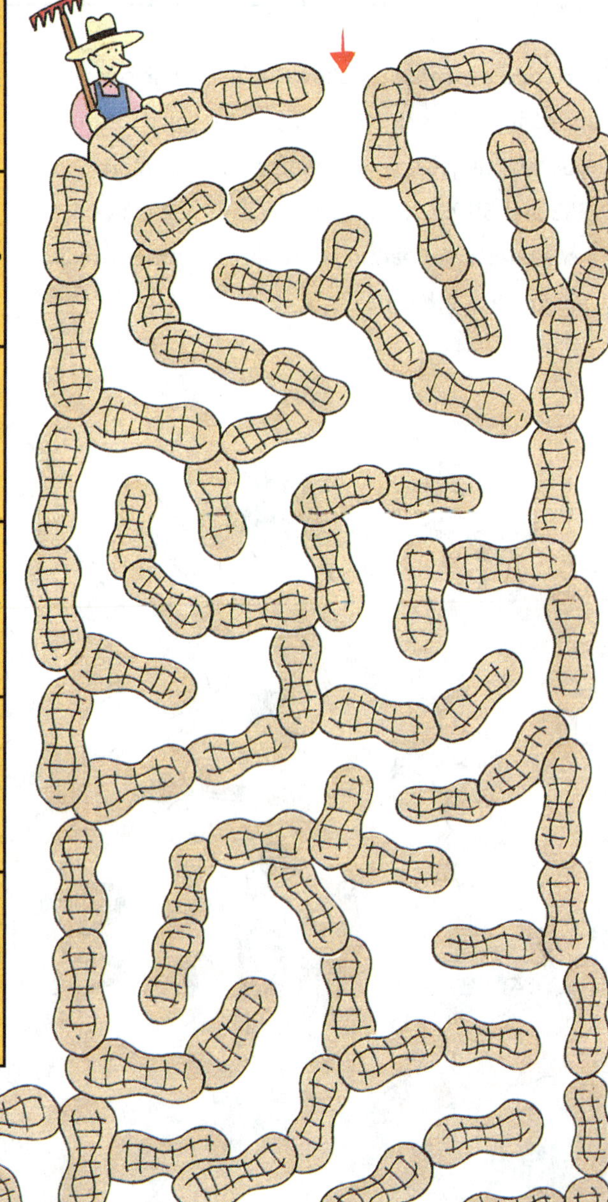

# Hawaii

Aloha State

Capital: Honolulu

Kukui (Candlenut) Yellow Hibiscus Nene (Hawaiian Goose)

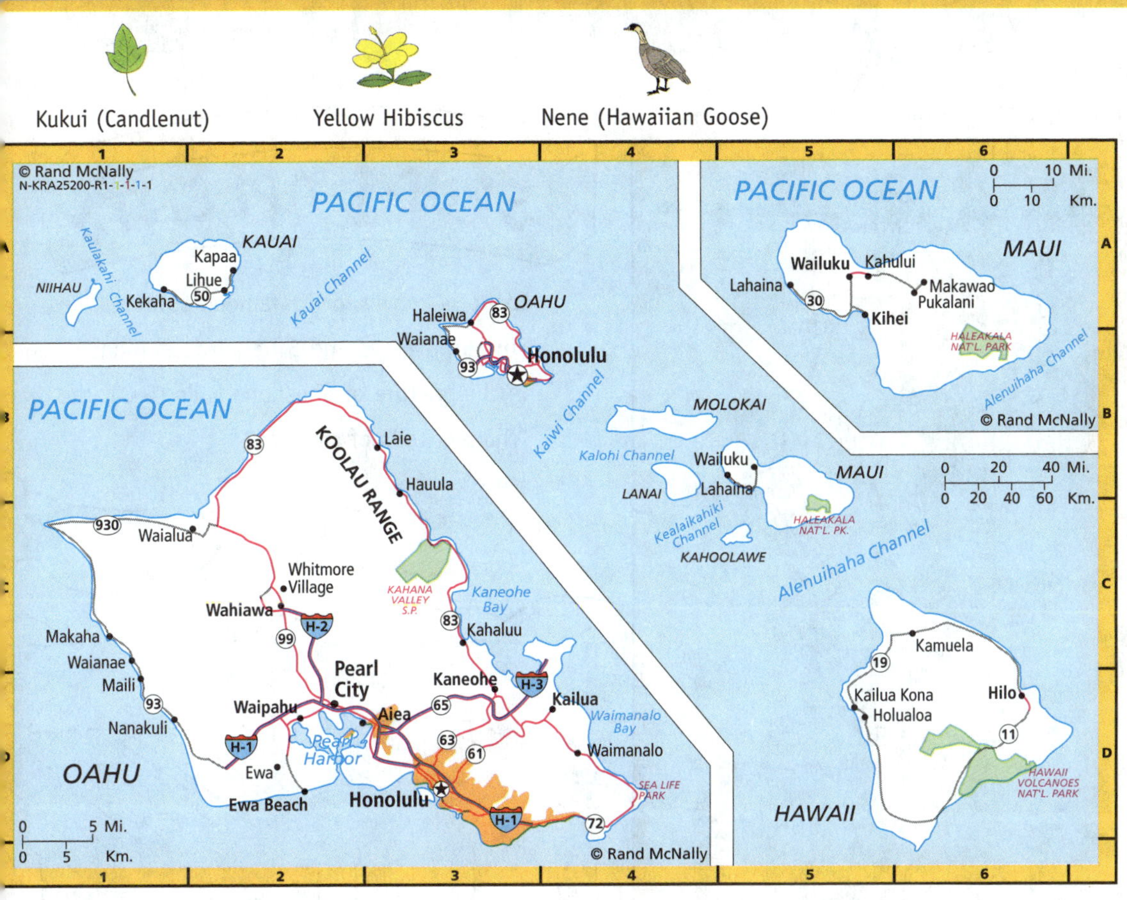

Connect the dots to find out what Kilauea is. Kilauea is in the National Park at coordinate D–6.

# IDaho

Gem State

Capital: Boise

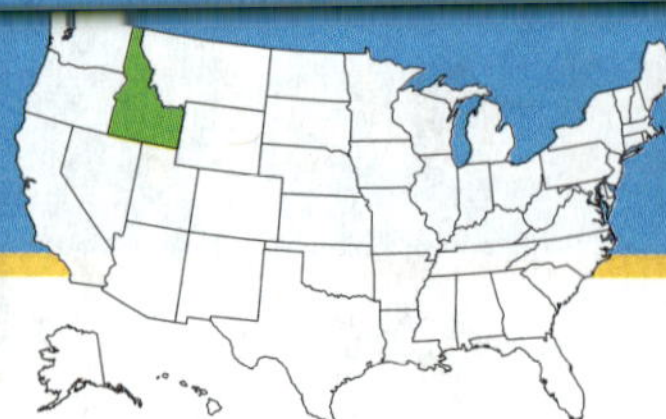

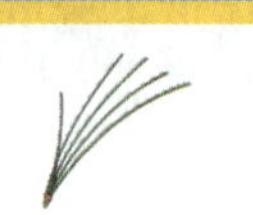

Western White Pine

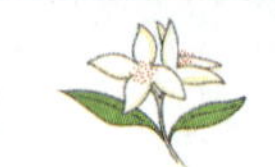

Syringa (Mock Orange)

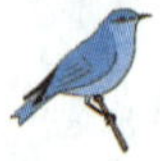
Mountain Bluebird

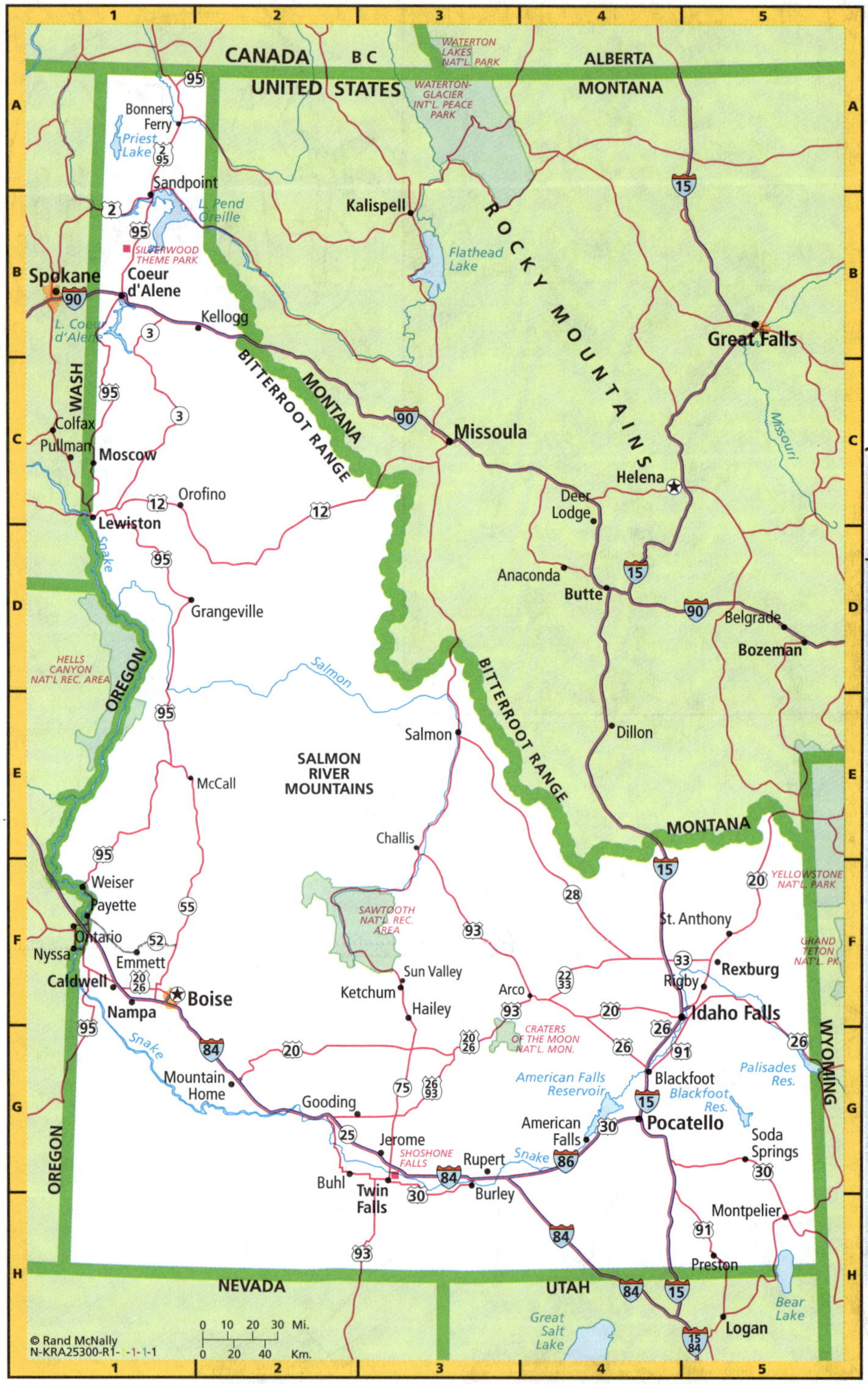


## SPUDS APLENTY

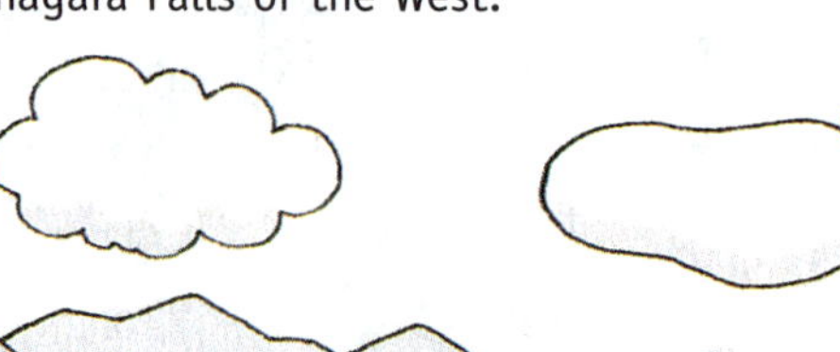

Idaho is known for its famous potatoes. Find 5 potatoes and 5 french fries hidden in this picture of Shoshone Falls (G-3), the "Niagara Falls of the West."

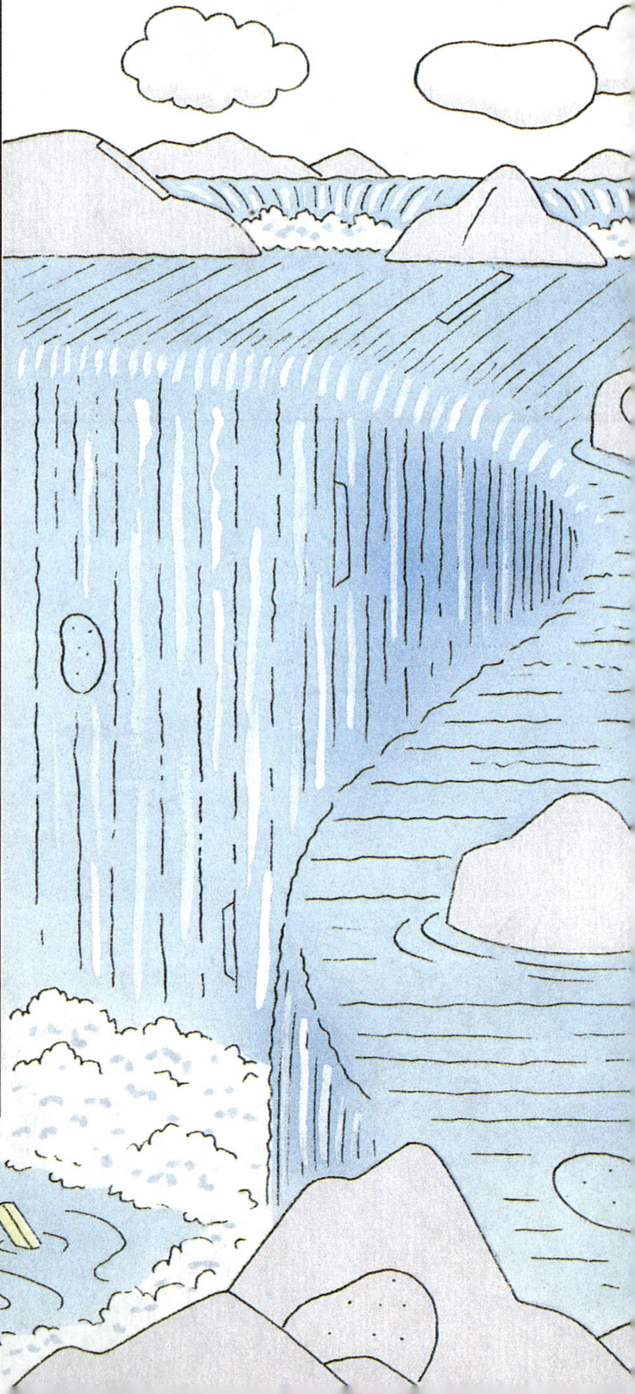

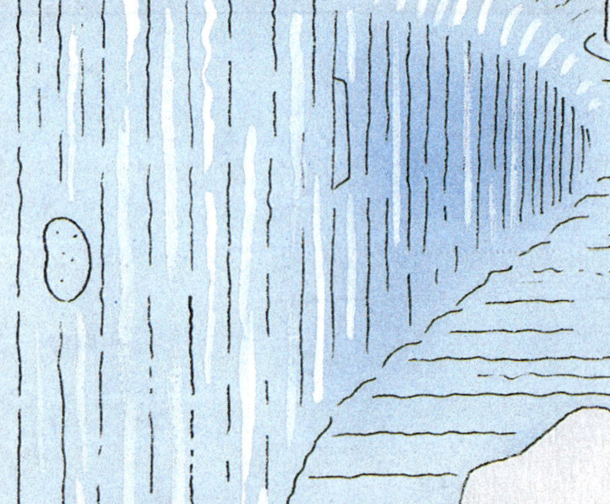

# Illinois

Prairie State

Capital: Springfield

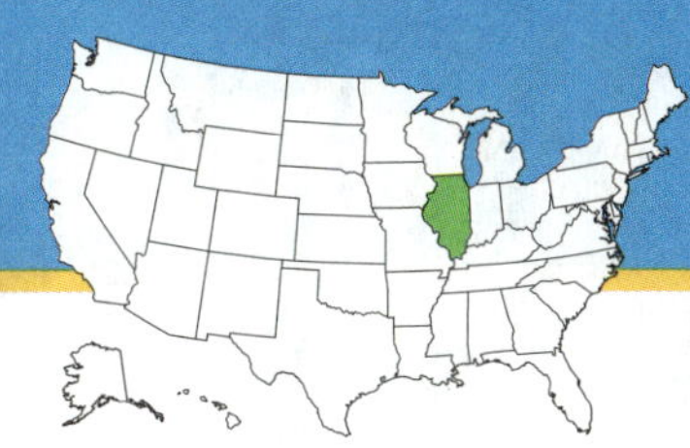

White Oak

Native Violet

Cardinal

## TOUR OF ILLINOIS

Follow the directions for a tour of Illinois.

Write the names of the cities you visit as you go.

1. ______________________

   A place to say, *"Bonjour"* (E–5)

2. ______________________

   A place for Santa Claus and Abraham Lincoln (D–2)

3. ______________________

   A place to have lunch (B–4)

4. ______________________

   A place to avoid (B–3)

5. ______________________

   A place to have an average time (C–4)

6. ______________________

   A place where a poor speller could celebrate (D–4)

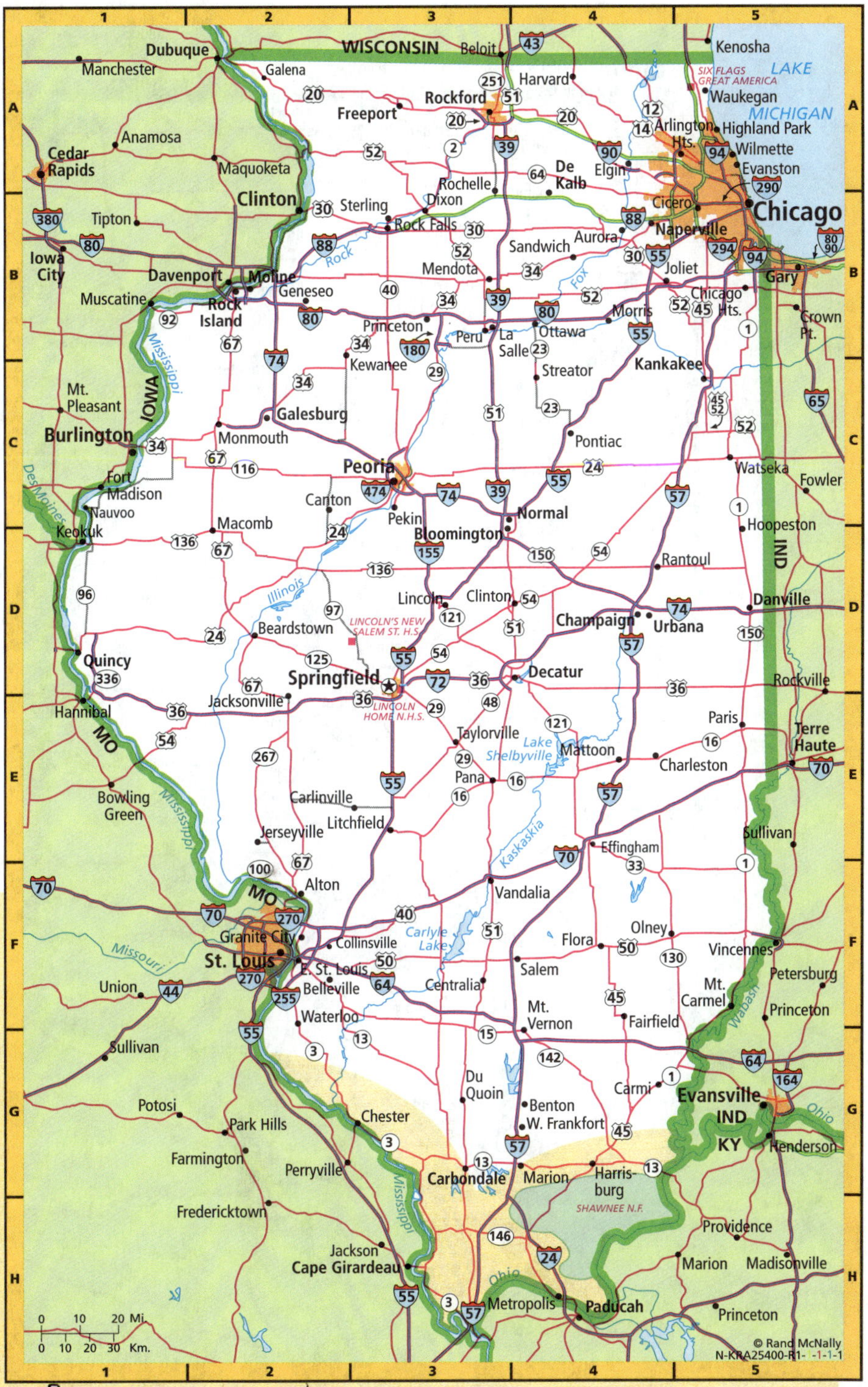

# INdiana

Hoosier State

Capital: Indianapolis

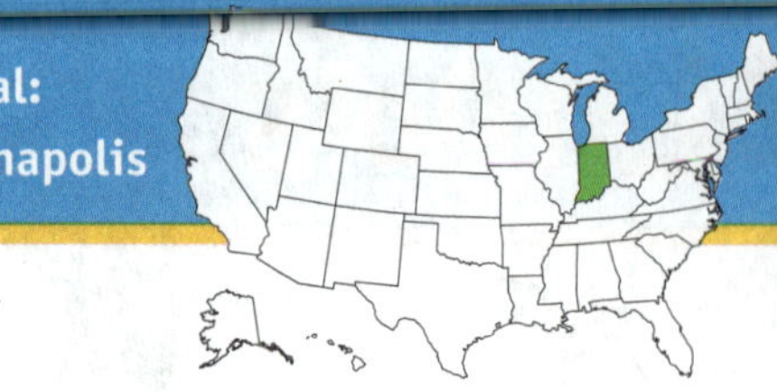

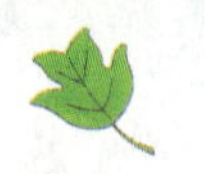

Tulip Tree

Peony

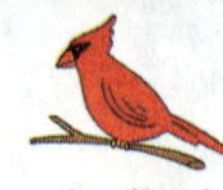

Cardinal

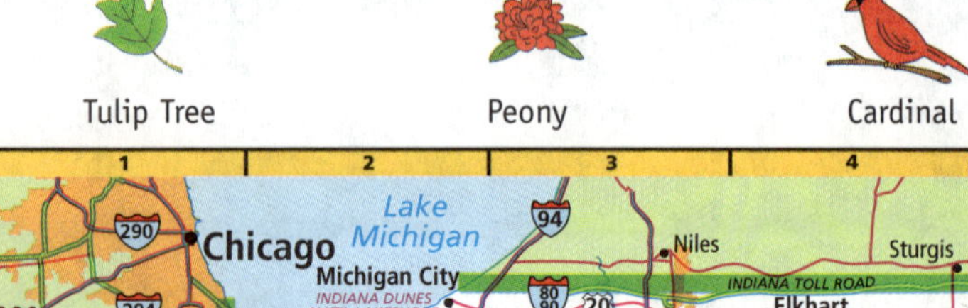

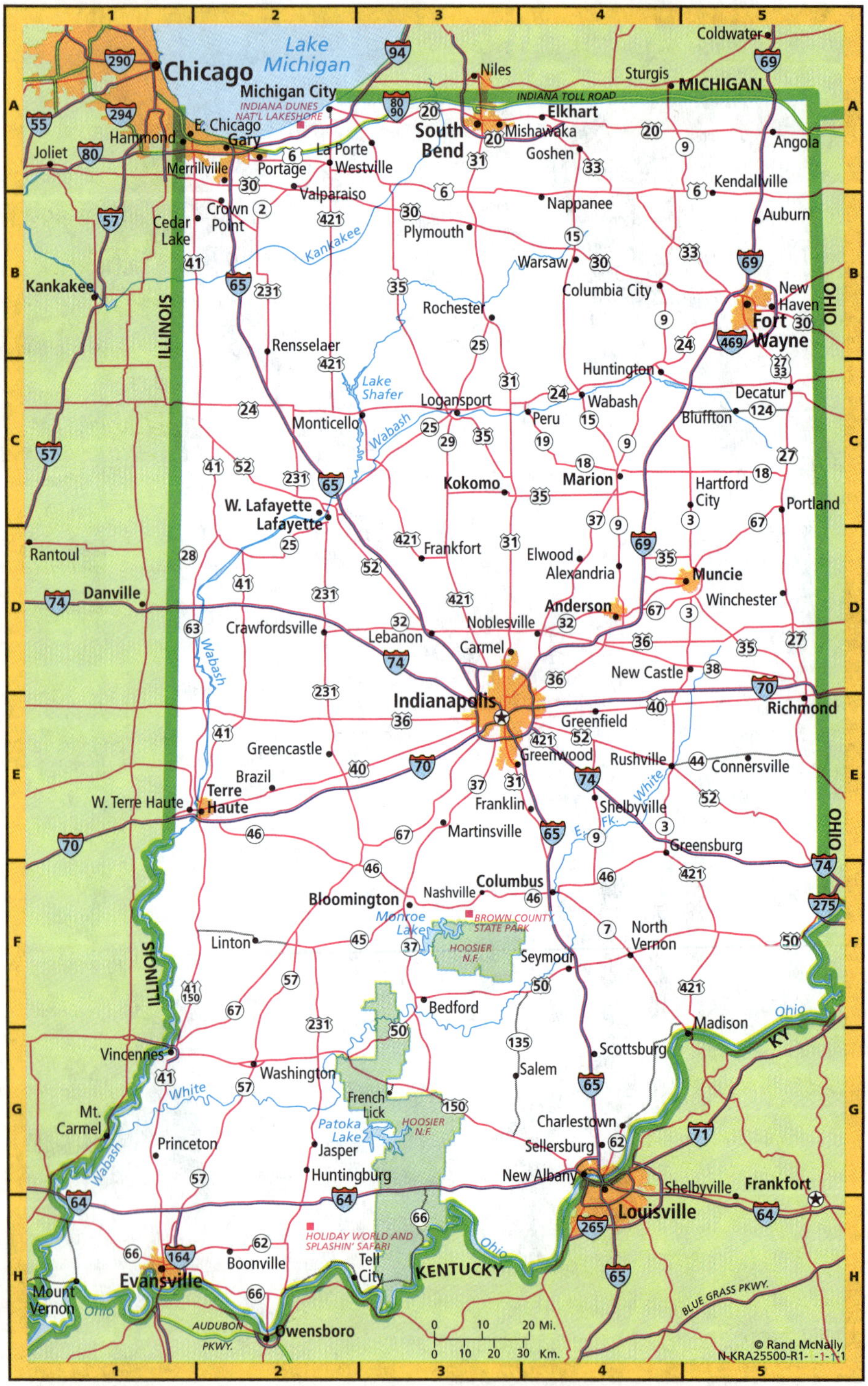


## A DAY AT THE RACES

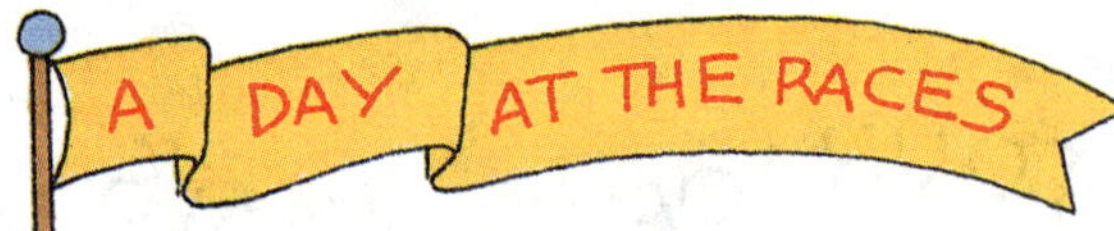

In the Indy 500 car race it can be hard to tell who is winning because some cars can be laps ahead of the others. Use the clues below to figure out which number car is winning and which cars are coming in 2nd and 3rd.

1. None of the odd numbered cars placed in the top three.
2. The black car didn't place.
3. The orange car did win.
4. The brown car didn't place.
5. The red car came in behind the orange car.

1st ______________________________

2nd ______________________________

3rd ______________________________

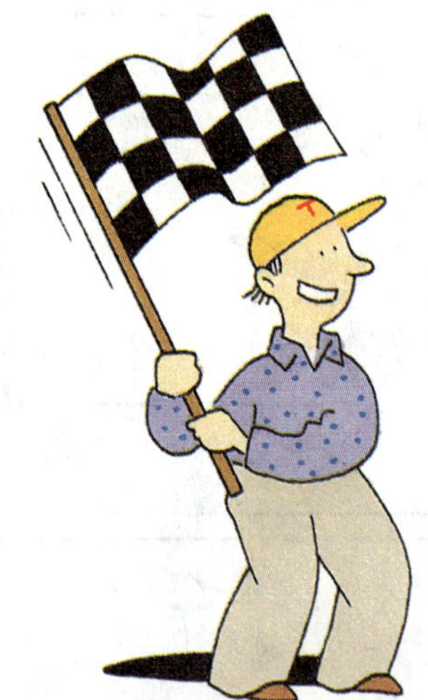

9
10
6
2
3
8
4
1
7

Hawkeye State

Capital: Des Moines

Oak
Wild Rose 
Eastern Goldfinch

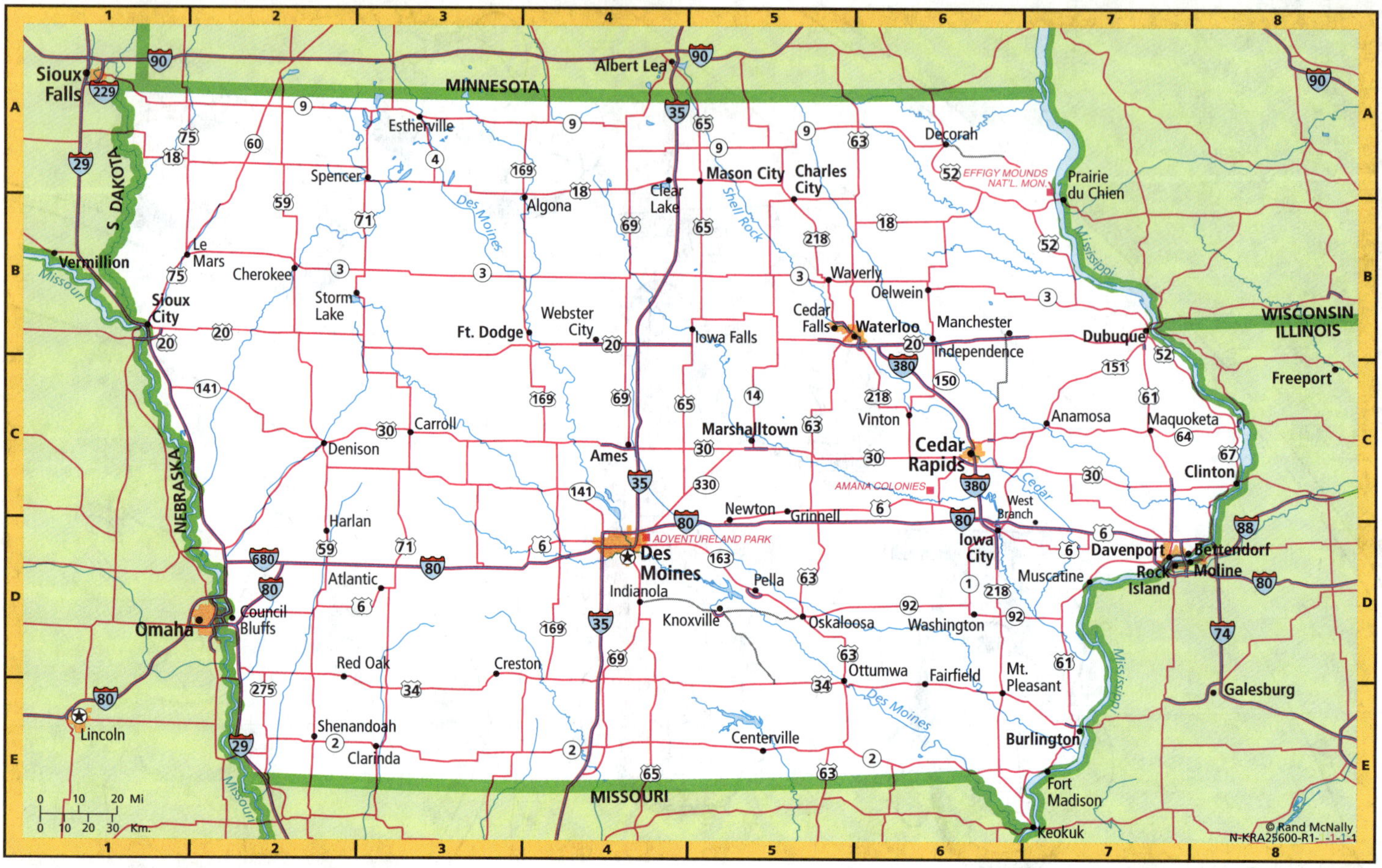

# FARM JUMBLE

The names of 7 farm animals are mixed up below. Unscramble them and write the correct names in the boxes. When you're done, the shaded letters, reading from top to bottom, will spell out the name of something that is made in Iowa. More of this product is made in Sioux City than in any other place in the world!

1. GIP
2. TROOSER
3. HEEPS
4. CWO
5. TOGA
6. RHOSE
7. NECKHIC

Sunflower State

Capital:
Topeka

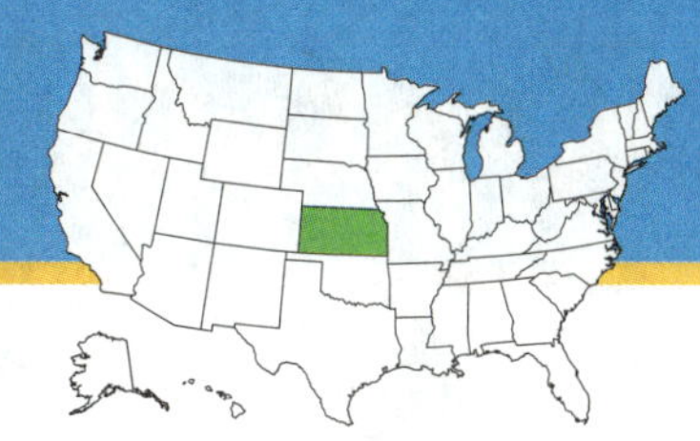

Cottonwood

Native Sunflower

Western Meadowlark

Dodge City, Kansas, was a famous town in the Old West.

Circle what doesn't belong in this Old West scene.

# Kentucky

Bluegrass State

Capital: Frankfort

Tulip Poplar

Goldenrod

Cardinal

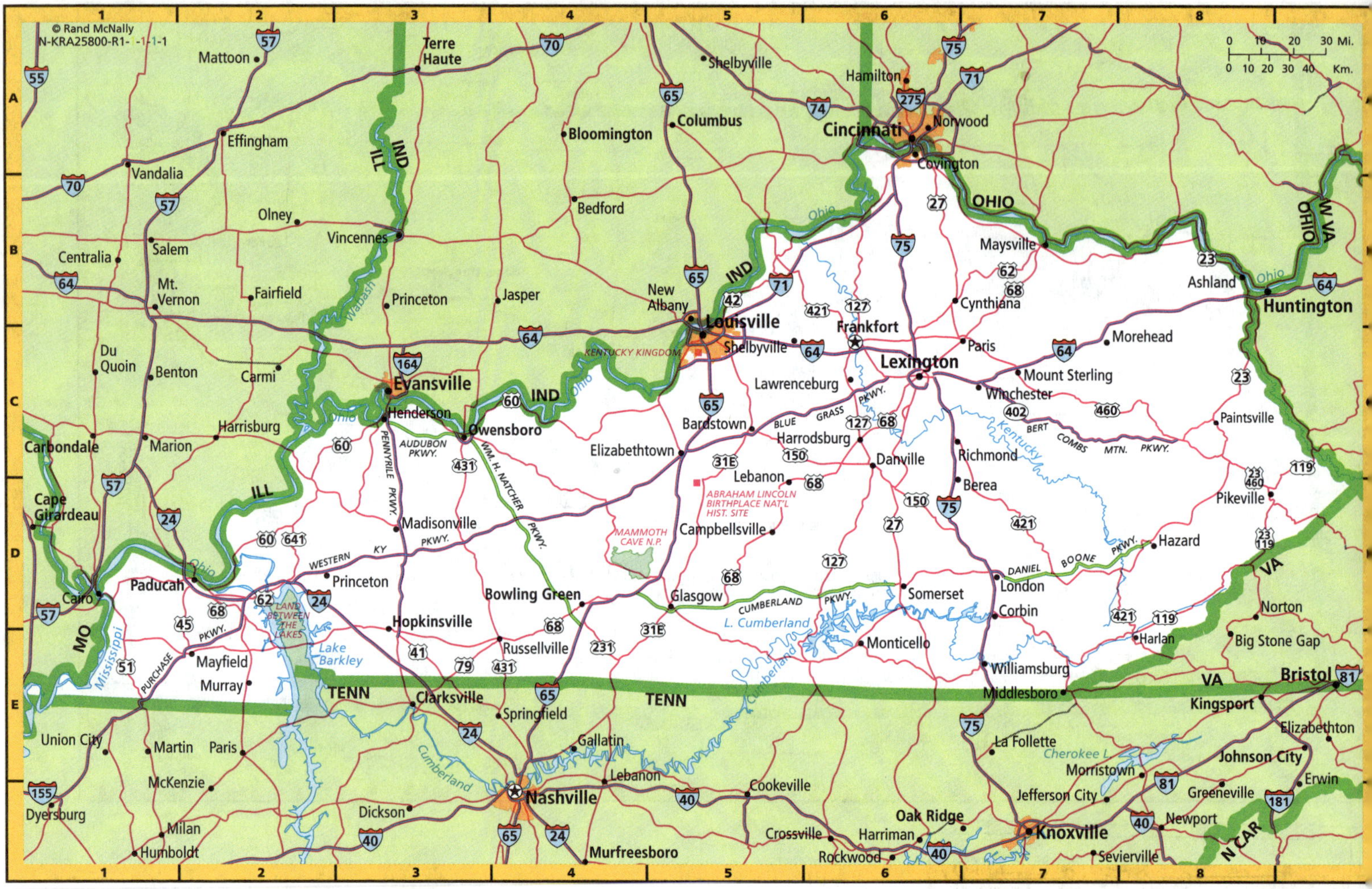

## Boy oh Boy!

The name "Ken" can be found in the first three letters of Kentucky.
How many boys' names can you find hidden in the cities on the map of Kentucky?

Hint: All of the names do not occur at the beginning.

# LouisiAna

Pelican State

Capital: Baton Rouge

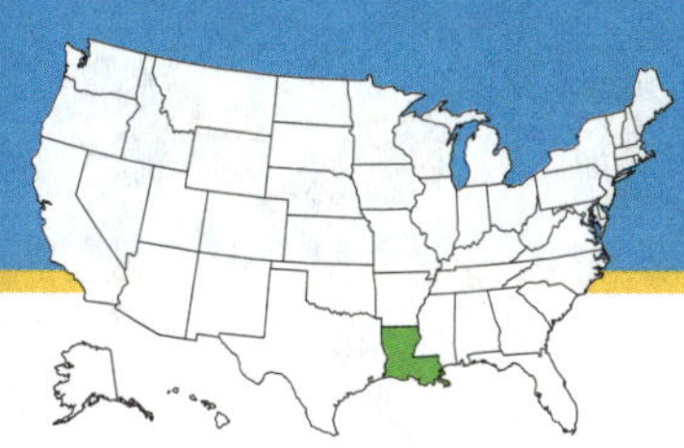

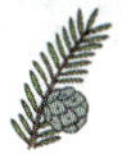

Bald Cypress

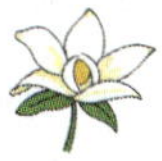

Magnolia

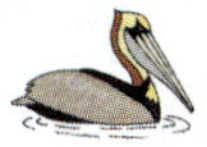

Eastern Brown Pelican

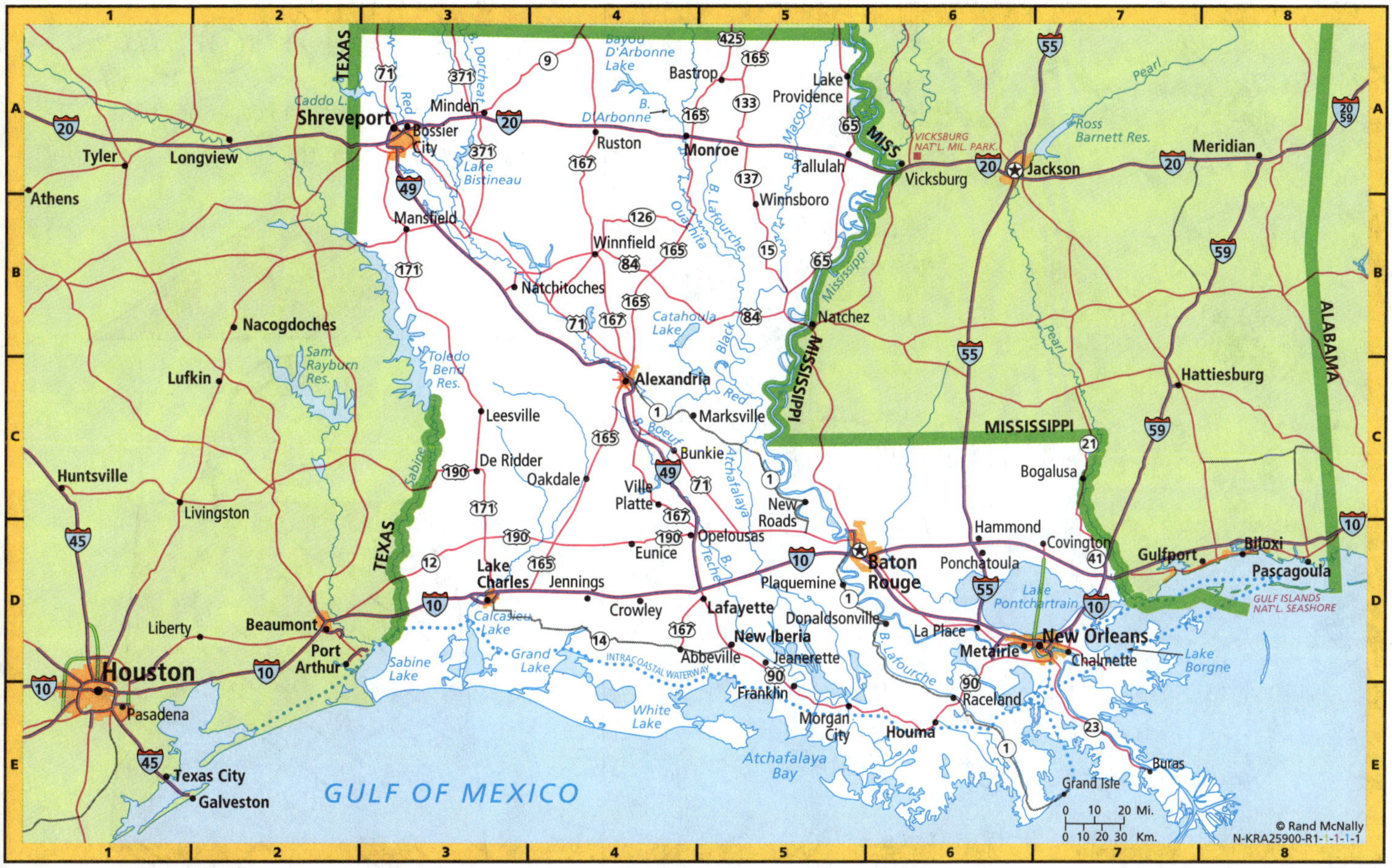

1 2 3 4 5 6 7 8
A B C D E
TEXAS
MISS
MISSISSIPPI
ALABAMA
GULF OF MEXICO
Shreveport
Bossier City
Minden
Caddo L.
Lake Bistineau
Ruston
D'Arbonne
Bayou D'Arbonne Lake
Bastrop
Monroe
Lake Providence
Tallulah
Winnsboro
Vicksburg
VICKSBURG NAT'L. MIL. PARK
Jackson
Ross Barnett Res.
Pearl
Meridian
Tyler
Longview
Athens
Mansfield
Winnfield
Natchitoches
Catahoula Lake
Natchez
Nacogdoches
Sam Rayburn Res.
Toledo Bend Res.
Lufkin
Alexandria
Marksville
Leesville
Hattiesburg
Bunkie
Ville Platte
De Ridder
Oakdale
Huntsville
Livingston
Bogalusa
New Roads
Opelousas
Eunice
Hammond
Covington
Baton Rouge
Ponchatoula
Gulfport
Biloxi
Pascagoula
Lake Charles
Jennings
Crowley
Lafayette
Plaquemine
Donaldsonville
Lake Pontchartrain
GULF ISLANDS NAT'L. SEASHORE
Liberty
Beaumont
Port Arthur
Calcasieu Lake
Sabine Lake
Grand Lake
New Iberia
Abbeville
Jeanerette
La Place
Metairie
New Orleans
Chalmette
Lake Borgne
Houston
Pasadena
White Lake
Franklin
Morgan City
Houma
Raceland
Atchafalaya Bay
Texas City
Galveston
Buras
Grand Isle
INTRACOASTAL WATERWAY
0 10 20 Mi.
0 10 20 30 Km.
© Rand McNally
N-KRA25900-R1-1-1-1-1


BIG RIVERS


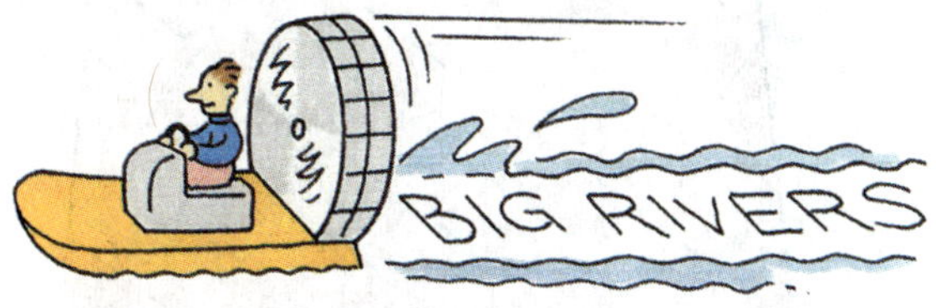

Can you fit the names of these Louisiana rivers, bayous, and lakes into the grid? One of the rivers is in the puzzle to get you started. Hint: Counting the number of letters in the words and using the color code will help.

**RIVERS:** Mississippi, Red, Ouachita, Sabine, Pearl, Atchafalaya, Black

**BAYOUS:** Teche, Lafourche, Macon, Boeuf, Dorcheat, D'Arbonne

**LAKES:** Pontchartrain, Calcasieu, White, Borgne Caddo, Bistineau, Toledo Bend Reservoir, Grand, Catahoula

B
O
R
G
N
E

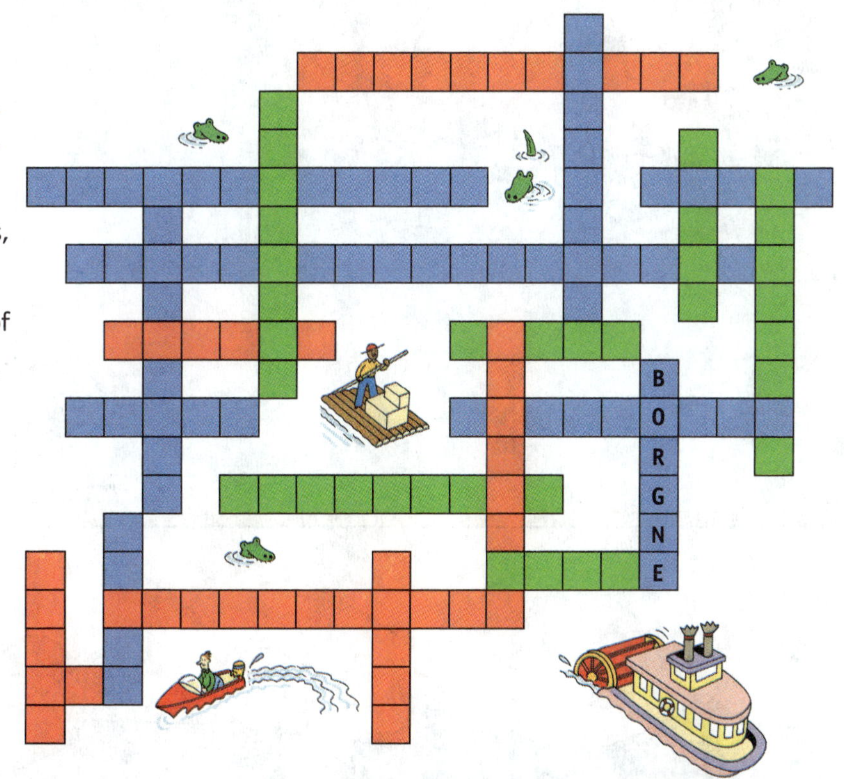

# MainE

Pine Tree State

Capital: Augusta

White Pine

White Pine Cone and Tassel

Chickadee

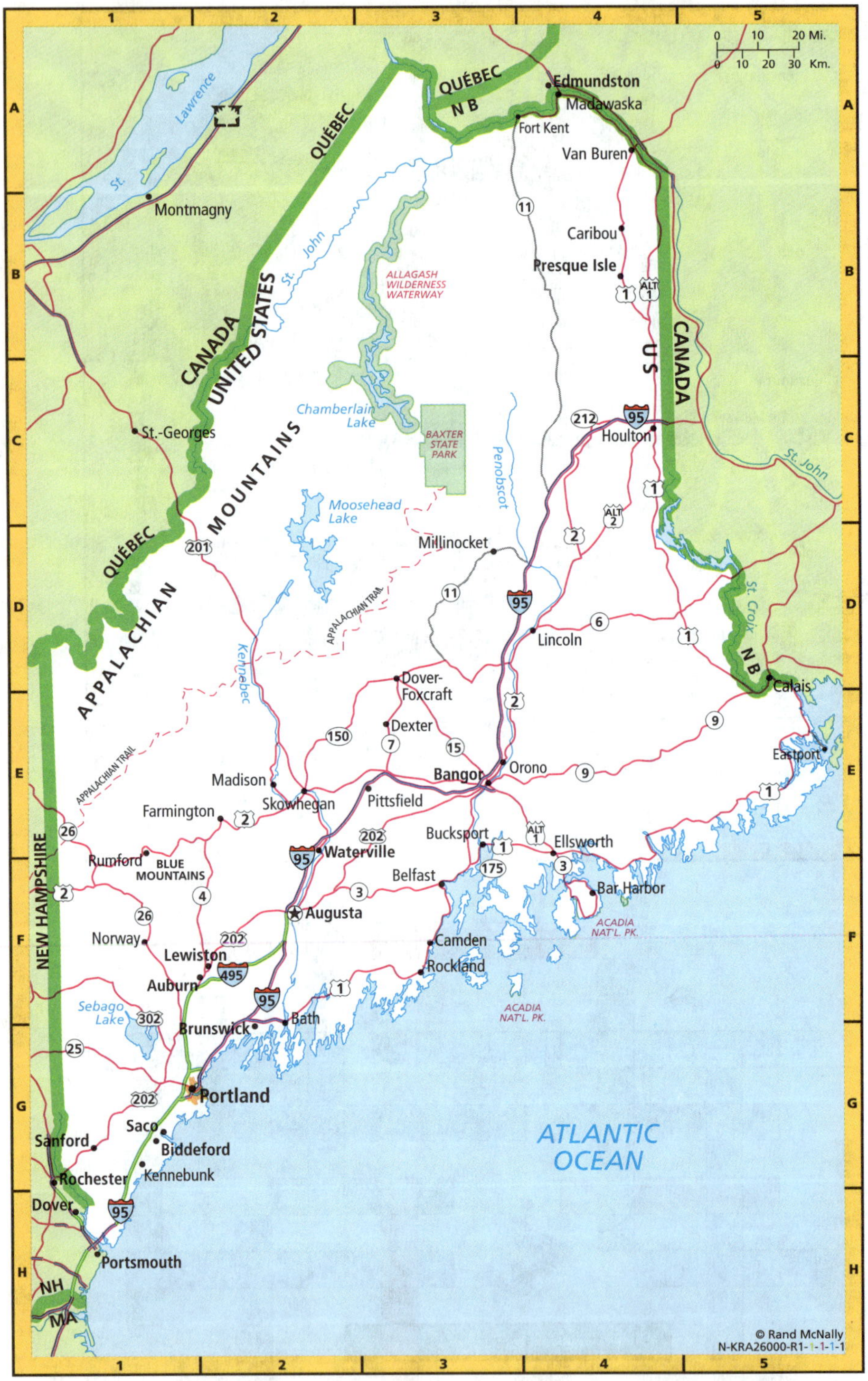

QUÉBEC
NB
Edmundston
Madawaska
Fort Kent
Van Buren
St. Lawrence
Montmagny
St. John
Caribou
Presque Isle
ALLAGASH WILDERNESS WATERWAY
CANADA
UNITED STATES
US
CANADA
Chamberlain Lake
BAXTER STATE PARK
Penobscot
Houlton
St.-Georges
MOUNTAINS
St. John
Moosehead Lake
Millinocket
QUÉBEC
APPALACHIAN
APPALACHIAN TRAIL
Lincoln
St. Croix
NB
Calais
Kennebec
Dover-Foxcroft
Dexter
Eastport
Madison
Bangor
Orono
APPALACHIAN TRAIL
Farmington
Skowhegan
Pittsfield
Bucksport
Ellsworth
NEW HAMPSHIRE
Rumford
BLUE MOUNTAINS
Waterville
Belfast
Bar Harbor
Augusta
ACADIA NAT'L. PK.
Norway
Lewiston
Camden
Rockland
Auburn
Sebago Lake
Brunswick
Bath
ACADIA NAT'L. PK.
Portland
Saco
Sanford
Biddeford
ATLANTIC OCEAN
Rochester
Kennebunk
Dover
Portsmouth
NH
MA


N-KRA26000-R1-1-1-1-1

# LiGHTS OUT!

Help the lighthouse keeper get to the top to warn the ships.

Old Line State

Capital: Annapolis

White Oak

Black-eyed Susan

Baltimore Oriole

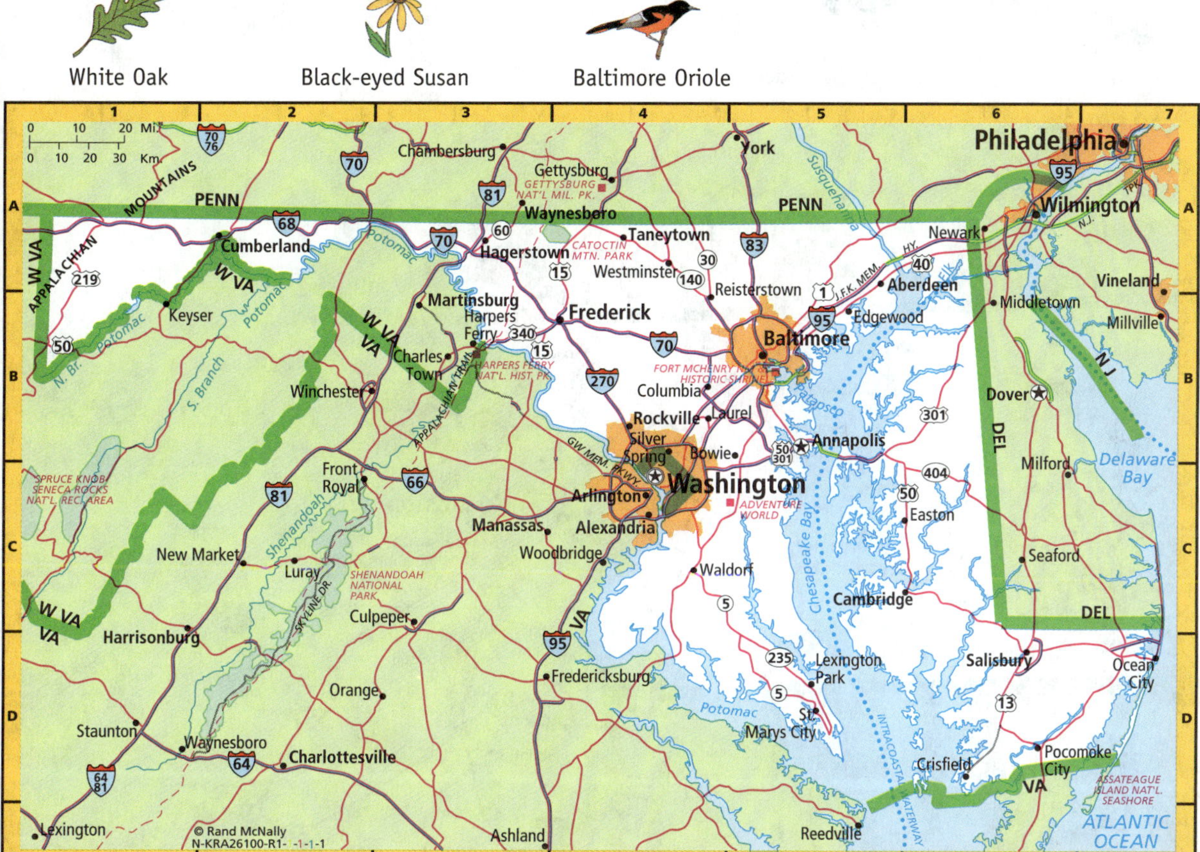

Francis Scott Key wrote the National Anthem in Maryland during the Battle of Baltimore in the War of 1812. Solve the code to find out where he was when he wrote these famous words.

1. Oh! Say can you see, by the dawn's early light,
2. what so proudly we hailed at the twilight's last gleaming?
3. Whose broad stripes and bright stars through the perilous fight,
4. o'er the ramparts we watched were so gallantly streaming?
5. And the rocket's red glare,
6. the bombs bursting in air
7. gave proof through the night
8. that our flag was still there.
9. Oh! Say does that star spangled banner yet wave
10. o'er the land of the free and the home of the brave?

Use the example at the right to understand the code. The letter G is in line number 1, word number 10, and letter number 3.

| G | |
|---|---|
| line | 1 |
| word | 10 |
| letter | 3 |

| H | | | | | | | | | | | | | | | |
|---|---|---|---|---|---|---|---|---|---|---|---|---|---|---|---|
| 9 | 7 | | 8 | 2 | 3 | 5 | | 2 | 4 | 4 | 2 | 4 | 7 | 5 | 5 |
| 1 | 4 | | 4 | 1 | 6 | 1 | | 3 | 3 | 9 | 8 | 1 | 5 | 5 | 4 |
| 2 | 3 | | 1 | 3 | 1 | 1 | | 1 | 1 | 7 | 9 | 1 | 1 | 5 | 1 |

| | | | | | | | | | | | | | | | .|
|---|---|---|---|---|---|---|---|---|---|---|---|---|---|---|---|
| 10 | 10 | | 8 | | 9 | 1 | 3 | 4 | 6 | 9 | 7 | | 2 | 3 | 4 | 7 |
| 9 | 3 | | 3 | | 7 | 9 | 3 | 3 | 4 | 2 | 3 | | 2 | 10 | 9 | 2 |
| 2 | 3 | | 3 | | 1 | 3 | 4 | 7 | 1 | 1 | 2 | | 1 | 4 | 7 | 1 |

# Massachusetts

Bay State

Capital: Boston

American Elm

Mayflower

Black-capped Chickadee

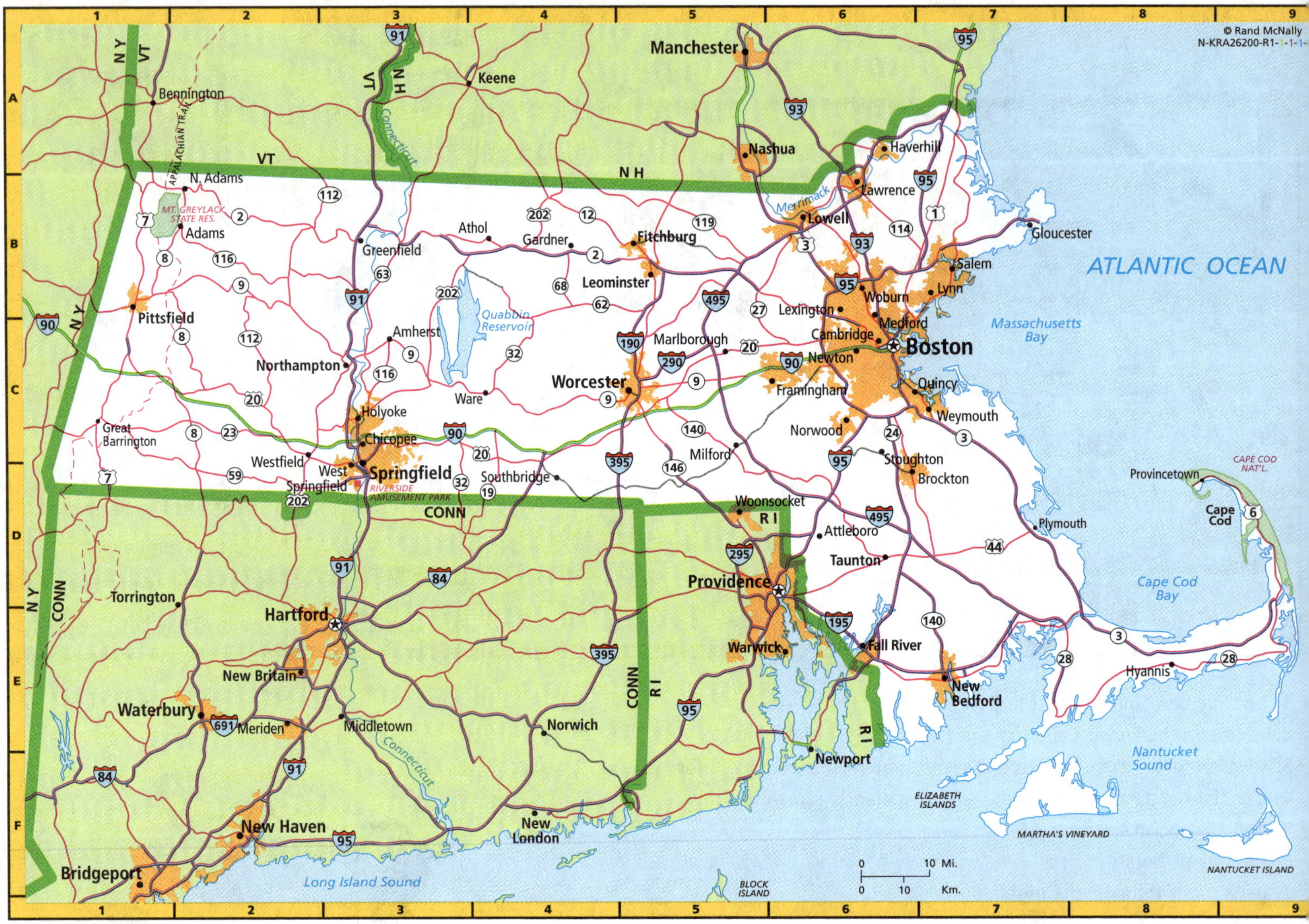

Many famous people were born and lived in Massachusetts. Fifteen of them are hidden in the word search below. Only the last names are hidden.

(JOHN) ADAMS
(LOUISA MAY) ALCOTT
(SUSAN B.) ANTHONY
(CLARA) BARTON
(EMILY) DICKINSON
(W.E.B.) DUBOIS
(RALPH WALDO) EMERSON
(BENJAMIN) FRANKLIN
(JOHN) HANCOCK
(OLIVER WENDELL) HOLMES
(WINSLOW) HOMER
(JOHN F.) KENNEDY
(EDGAR ALLAN) POE
(PAUL) REVERE
(NORMAN) ROCKWELL

A D R L P O E

E X I H O L M E S

F A N C D E C E R E

G R R K A H M K R A

M B A I R E E E W H

L S L N R E V H A E N

K E I S K E M N N O L A

N E O O R L C O T R L L

N N N B O I R H C Y

D N C U A N O A

V K E B D T N I D

T H O D T R Y E A

A D A M S Y U

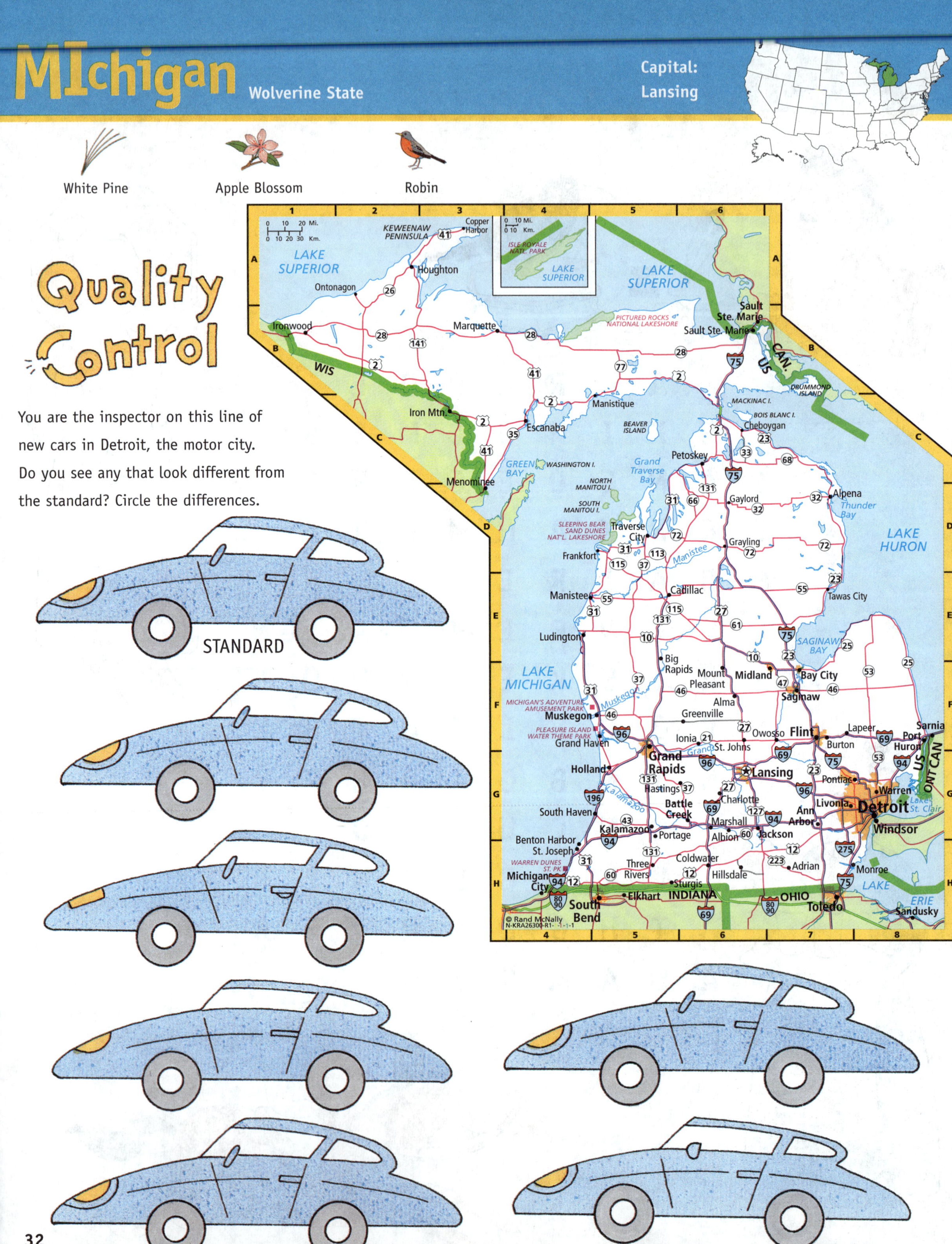

MIchigan
Wolverine State
Capital:
Lansing
White Pine
Apple Blossom
Robin
Quality Control
You are the inspector on this line of new cars in Detroit, the motor city. Do you see any that look different from the standard? Circle the differences.
STANDARD
LAKE SUPERIOR
KEWEENAW PENINSULA
Copper Harbor
Houghton
Ontonagon
Ironwood
Marquette
Iron Mtn.
Escanaba
Menominee
WIS
ISLE ROYALE NATL. PARK
PICTURED ROCKS NATIONAL LAKESHORE
Sault Ste. Marie
CAN.
US
DRUMMOND ISLAND
MACKINAC I.
BOIS BLANC I.
Cheboygan
Manistique
BEAVER ISLAND
GREEN BAY
WASHINGTON I.
Grand Traverse Bay
Petoskey
Gaylord
Alpena
Thunder Bay
NORTH MANITOU I.
SOUTH MANITOU I.
SLEEPING BEAR SAND DUNES NAT'L. LAKESHORE
Traverse City
Frankfort
Grayling
Manistee
LAKE HURON
Cadillac
Tawas City
Ludington
SAGINAW BAY
LAKE MICHIGAN
Big Rapids
Mount Pleasant
Midland
Bay City
Saginaw
Alma
MICHIGAN'S ADVENTURE AMUSEMENT PARK
Muskegon
Greenville
PLEASURE ISLAND WATER THEME PARK
Grand Haven
Ionia
St. Johns
Owosso
Flint
Lapeer
Port Huron
Sarnia
Burton
Grand Rapids
Holland
Lansing
Pontiac
Hastings
Charlotte
Warren
South Haven
Battle Creek
Livonia
Detroit
Ann Arbor
Lake St. Clair
Marshall
Windsor
Kalamazoo
Portage
Albion
Jackson
Benton Harbor
St. Joseph
WARREN DUNES ST. PK
Three Rivers
Coldwater
Adrian
Monroe
Hillsdale
Michigan City
Sturgis
South Bend
Elkhart
INDIANA
OHIO
Toledo
LAKE ERIE
Sandusky
ONT. CAN
© Rand McNally

# MiNnesota

North Star State

Capital: St. Paul

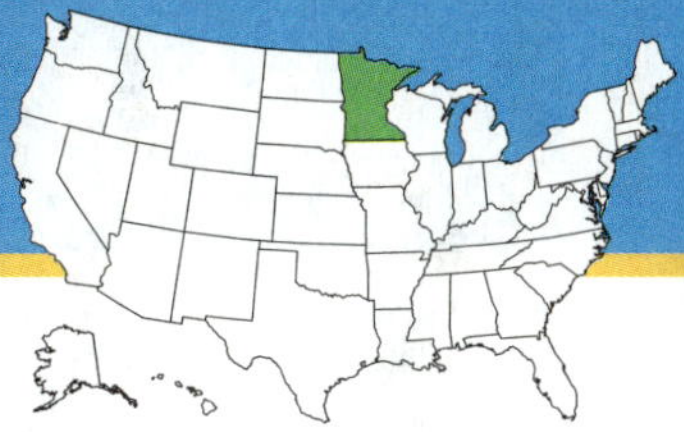

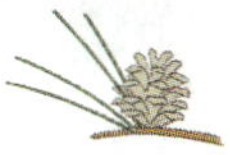

Norway Pine

Pink-and-white Lady's Slipper

Common Loon

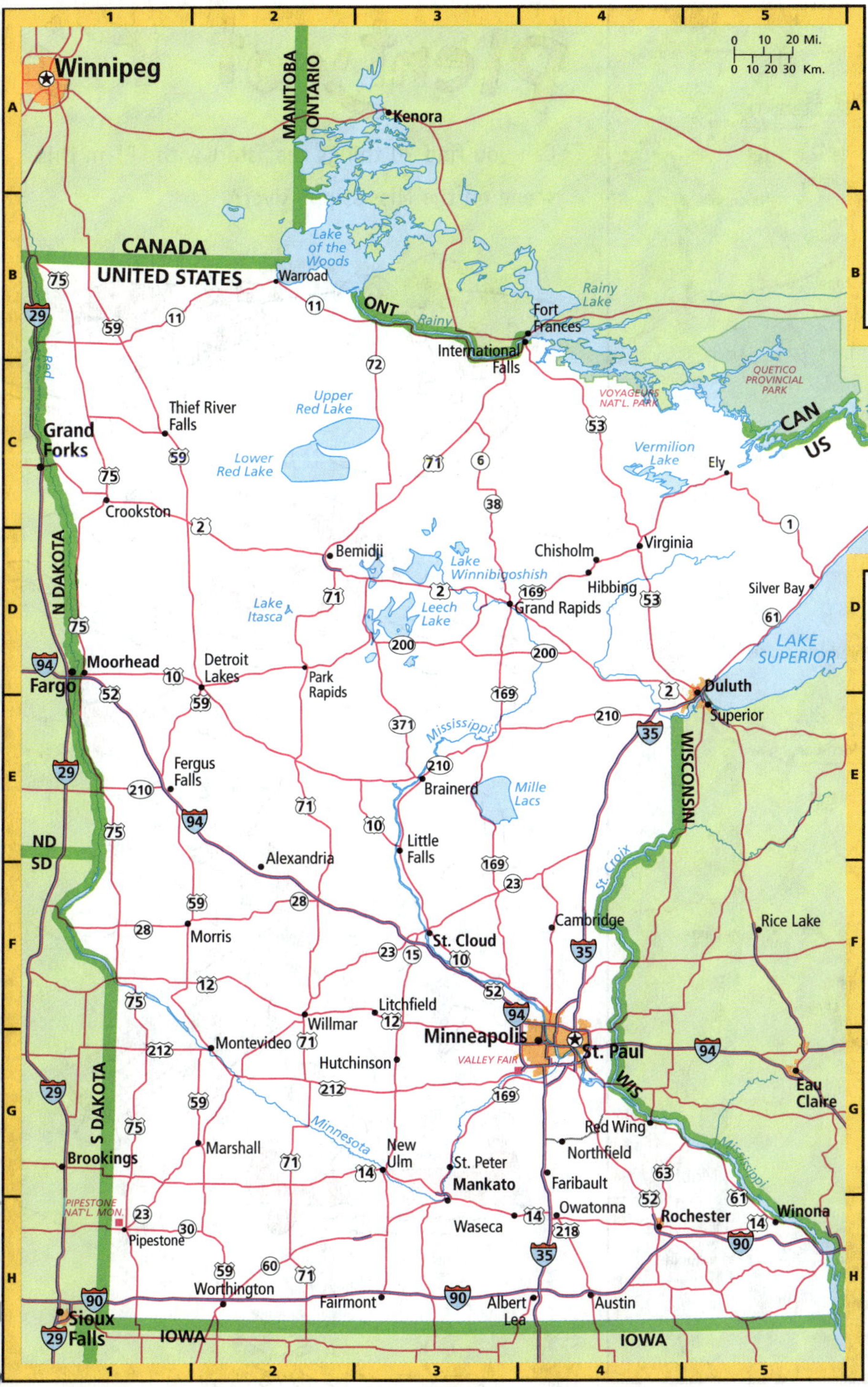

LOTSA LAKES

Minnesota is called the land of 10,000 lakes. Use the coordinates and clues to find a few of these lakes.

ACROSS
3. E-3; unscramble LIMEL
4. C-5; has 1,000,000 in it
6. D-3; hope not to find these in lake

DOWN
1. C-3; above and rosy
2. D-3; 14 letters in this name
5. D-2; unscramble ASTICA
6. C-2; below and rosy

# Mississippi

Magnolia State

Capital:
Jackson

Magnolia

Magnolia

Mockingbird

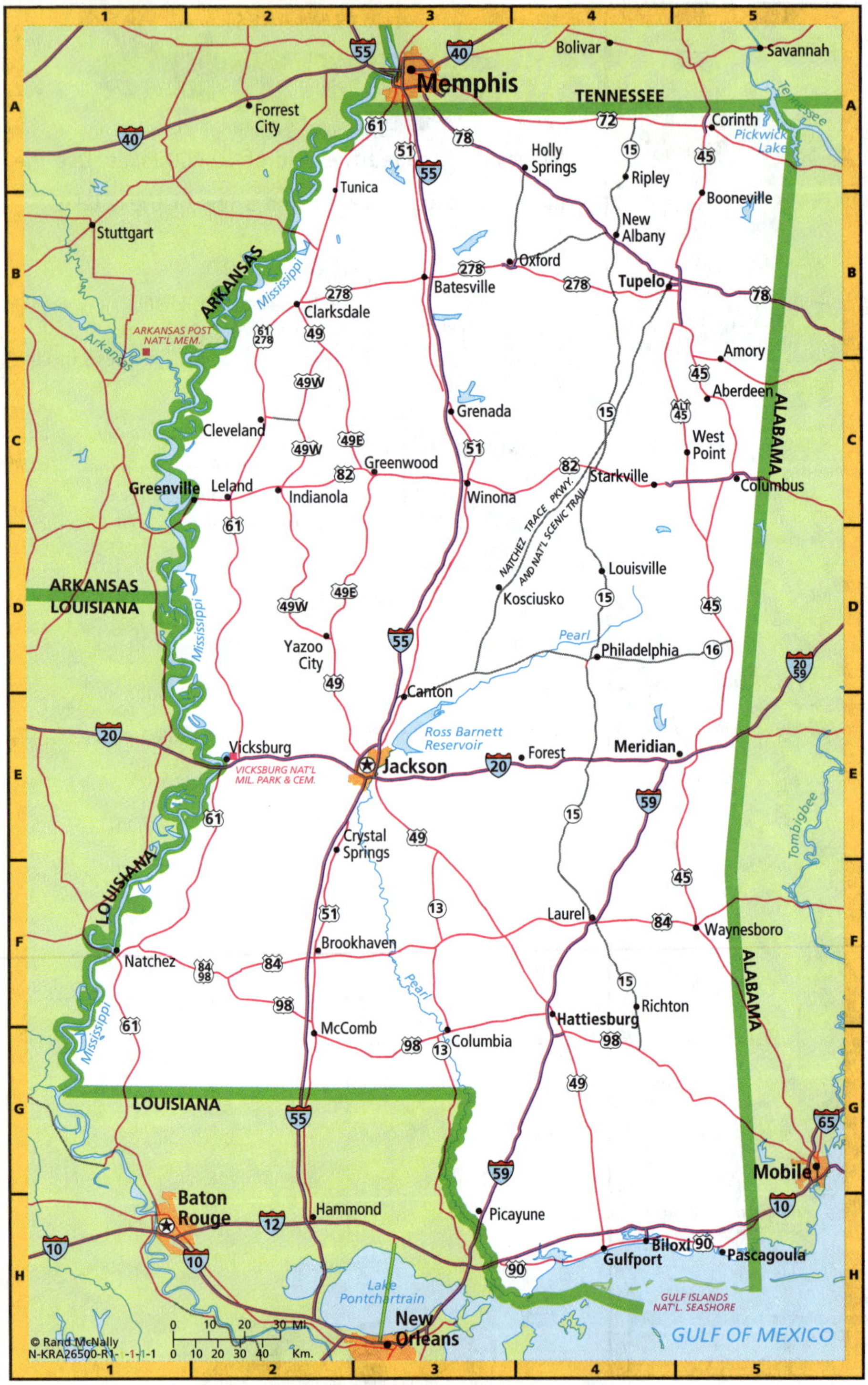

1 2 3 4 5
A B C D E F G H

Memphis
TENNESSEE
Bolivar
Savannah
Forrest City
Corinth
Pickwick Lake
Tennessee
Holly Springs
Ripley
Tunica
Booneville
Stuttgart
New Albany
Oxford
Batesville
Tupelo
ARKANSAS
Mississippi
Clarksdale
ARKANSAS POST NAT'L MEM.
Arkansas
Amory
Aberdeen
Grenada
West Point
Cleveland
ALABAMA
Greenwood
Starkville
Greenville
Leland
Indianola
Winona
Columbus
NATCHEZ TRACE PKWY. AND NAT'L SCENIC TRAIL
Louisville
ARKANSAS
LOUISIANA
Kosciusko
Yazoo City
Pearl
Philadelphia
Canton
Ross Barnett Reservoir
Vicksburg
VICKSBURG NAT'L MIL. PARK & CEM.
Jackson
Forest
Meridian
Crystal Springs
Tombigbee
LOUISIANA
Laurel
Waynesboro
Natchez
Brookhaven
ALABAMA
Richton
McComb
Hattiesburg
Columbia
LOUISIANA
Mobile
Baton Rouge
Hammond
Picayune
Biloxi
Gulfport
Pascagoula
Lake Pontchartrain
New Orleans
GULF ISLANDS NAT'L. SEASHORE
GULF OF MEXICO
0 10 20 30 Mi.
0 10 20 30 40 Km.
© Rand McNally
N-KRA26500-R1- -1-I-1

# Plenty of P's

Can you find 20 things that start with "P" in this scene on the Mississippi River?

# Missouri

Show Me State

Capital: Jefferson City

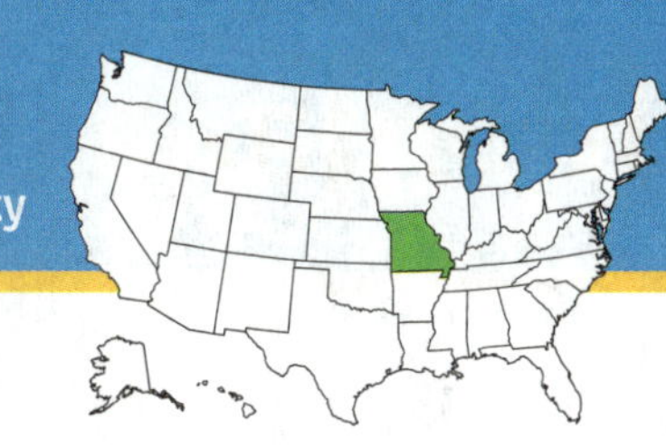

Flowering Dogwood    Hawthorn Blossom    Bluebird

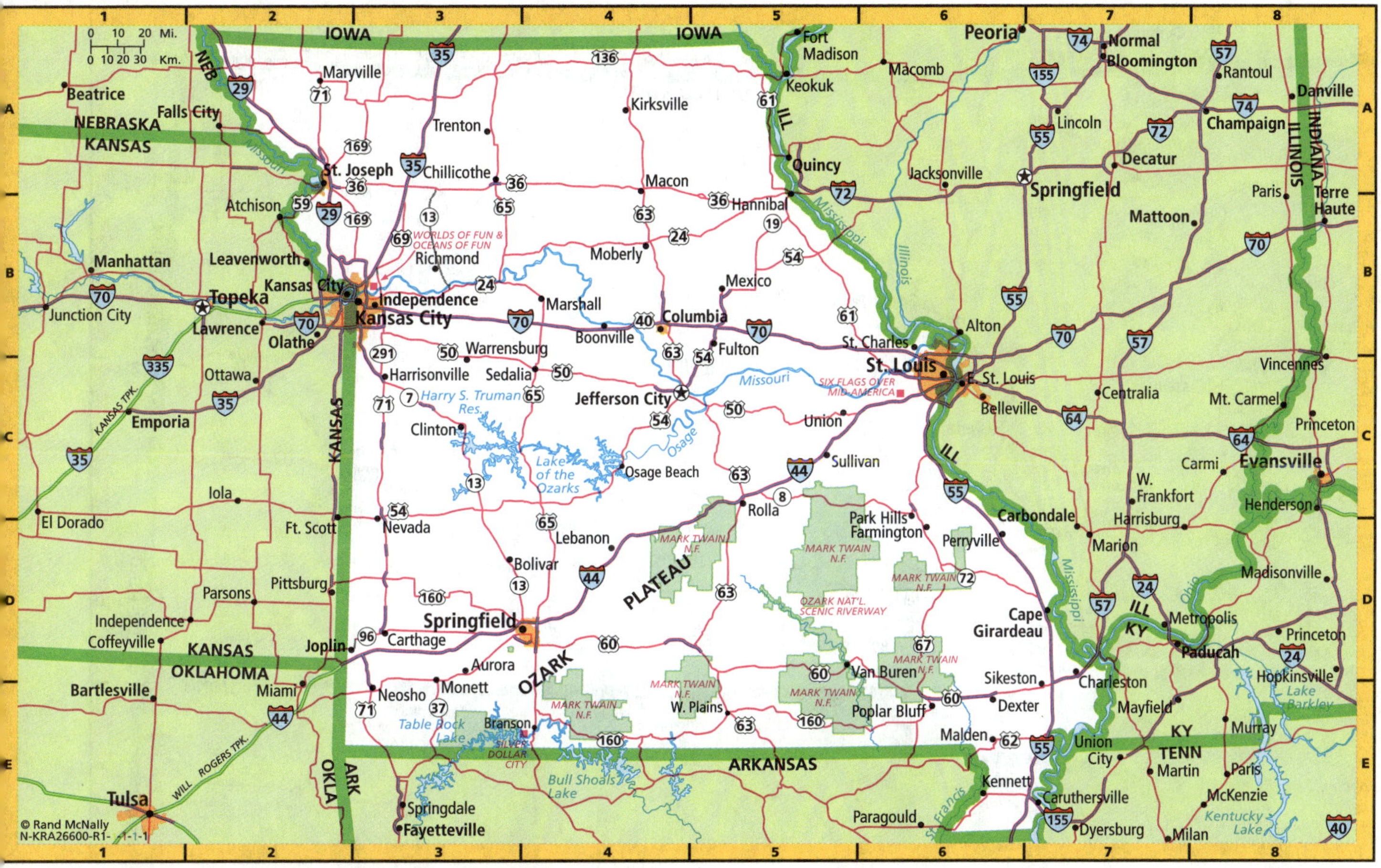

## BORDER PATROL

Eight states share borders with Missouri. Can you fit the names of the bordering states into the puzzle?

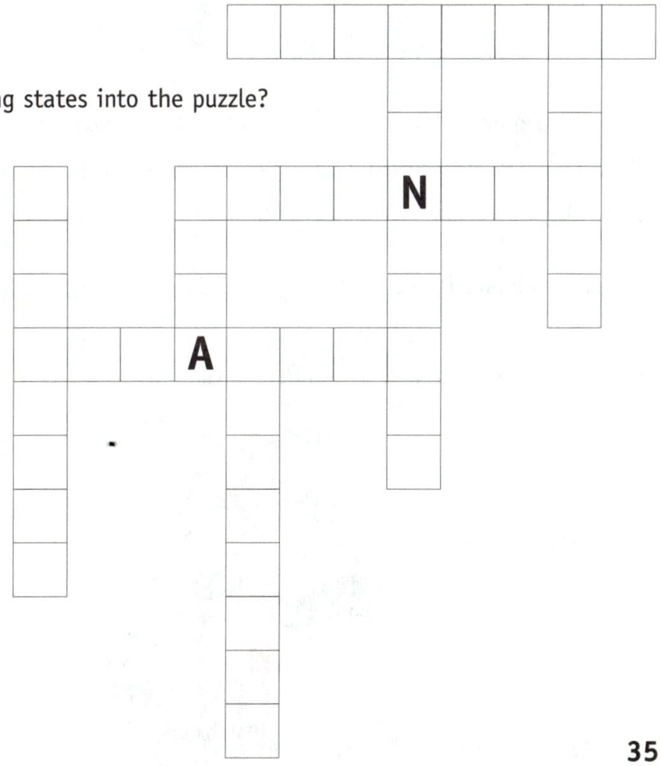

N

A

# Montana

Treasure State

Capital:
Helena

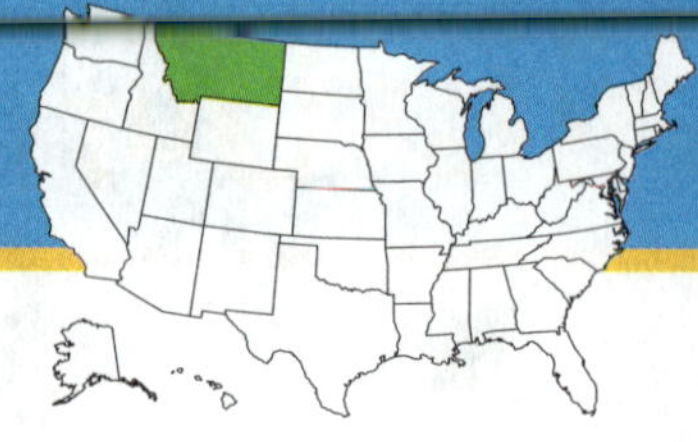

Ponderosa Pine

Bitterroot

Western Meadowlark

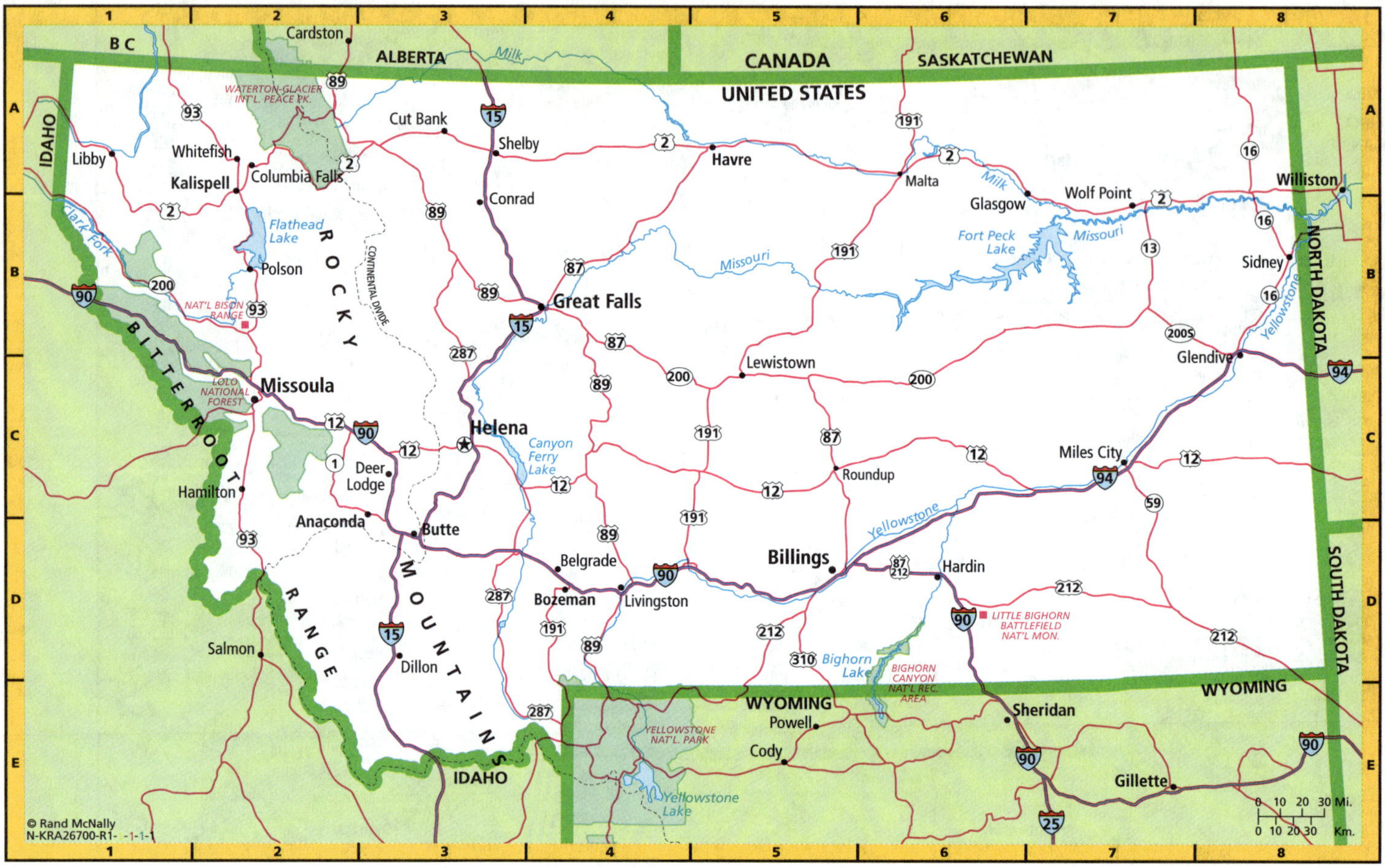

1 2 3 4 5 6 7 8
A B C D E

BC
ALBERTA
CANADA
SASKATCHEWAN
UNITED STATES
IDAHO
NORTH DAKOTA
SOUTH DAKOTA
WYOMING
Cardston
WATERTON-GLACIER INT'L. PEACE PK.
Milk
Cut Bank
Shelby
Havre
Malta
Glasgow
Wolf Point
Williston
Libby
Whitefish
Columbia Falls
Kalispell
Conrad
Flathead Lake
Polson
Fort Peck Lake
Missouri
Sidney
Clark Fork
NAT'L BISON RANGE
ROCKY
CONTINENTAL DIVIDE
Great Falls
Yellowstone
Glendive
BITTERROOT
LOLO NATIONAL FOREST
Missoula
Lewistown
Helena
Canyon Ferry Lake
Deer Lodge
Hamilton
Roundup
Miles City
Anaconda
Butte
Billings
Belgrade
Hardin
MOUNTAINS
RANGE
Bozeman
Livingston
LITTLE BIGHORN BATTLEFIELD NAT'L MON.
Salmon
Dillon
Bighorn Lake
BIGHORN CANYON NAT'L REC. AREA
Powell
Sheridan
YELLOWSTONE NAT'L PARK
Cody
Yellowstone Lake
Gillette
0 10 20 30 Mi.
0 10 20 30 Km.

© Rand McNally
N-KRA26700-R1- -1-1-1

# SNOWBOARD SHUFFLE

After a morning of boarding at Big Sky, this snowboarder went in for lunch. When he came out, he couldn't remember where he put his snowboard. Using the clues that he recalls, help him find his board.

1. His snowboard isn't next to a pair of skis.
2. His snowboard is not blue.
3. His snowboard is next to a blue snowboard.

# NEbraska

Cornhusker State

Capital: Lincoln

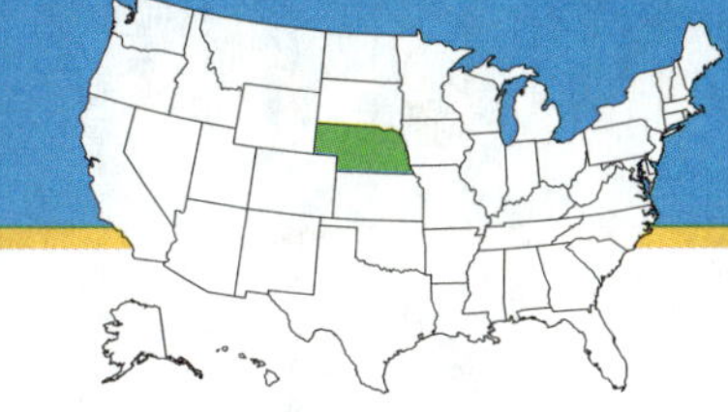

Cottonwood

Goldenrod

Western Meadowlark

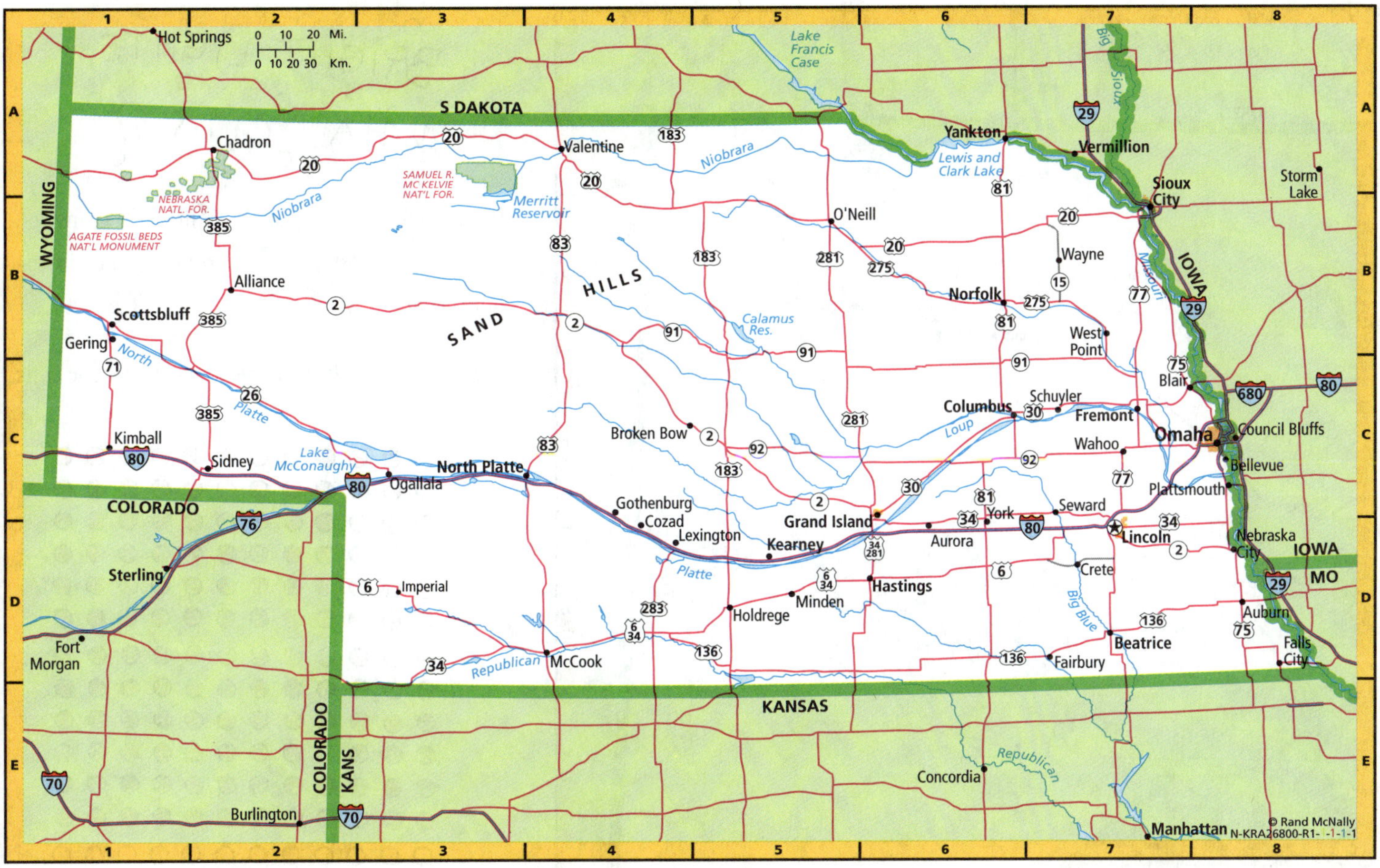

# Thrown for a Loop

The cowboy tradition is alive and kicking in Nebraska. Here, a few cowboys have been practicing their roping tricks. Some of the ropes lying on the ground will form knots when both ends are pulled. Can you tell which ones?

Silver State

Capital: Carson City

Single-leaf Pinon

Sagebrush

Mountain Bluebird

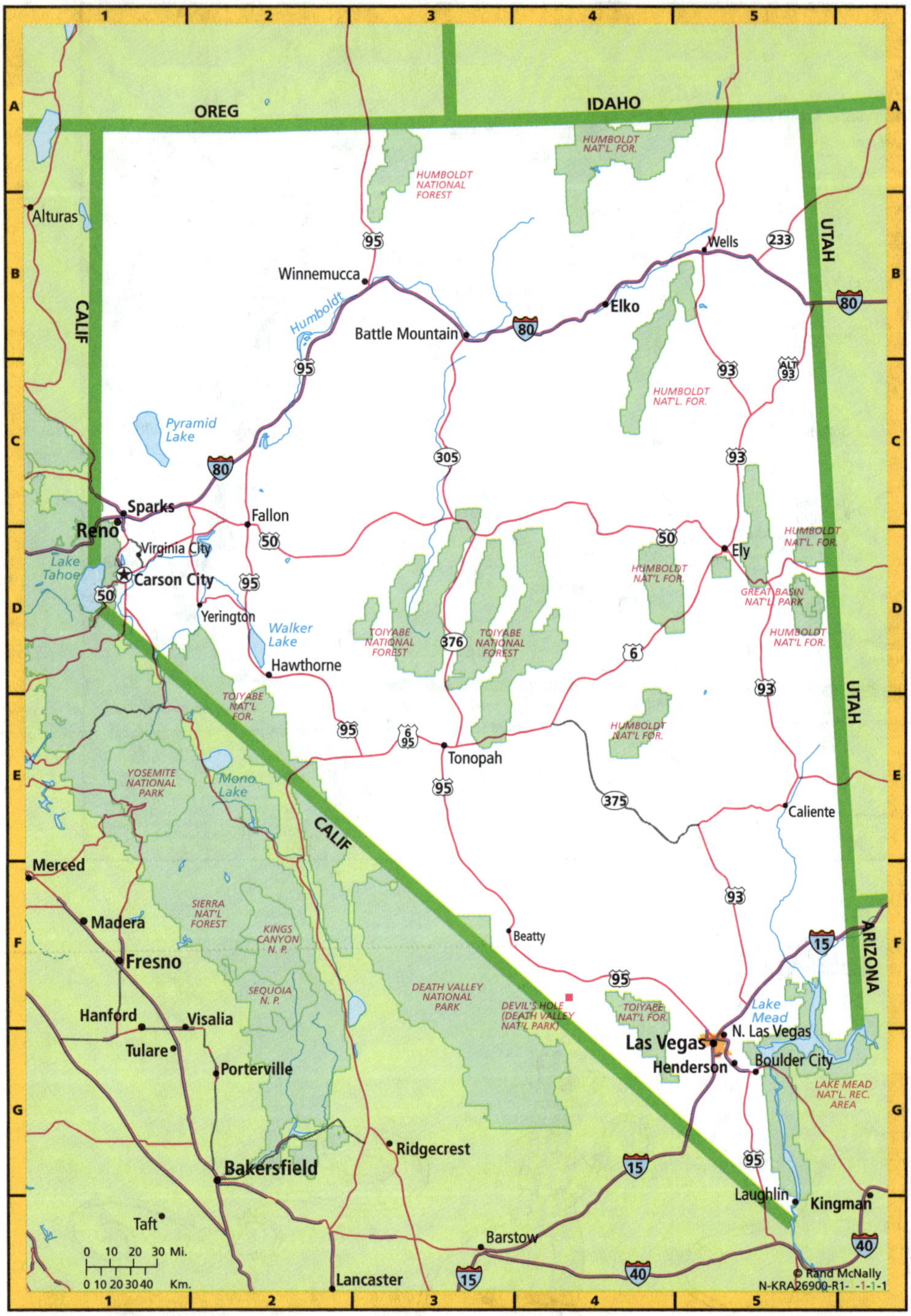

Hidden within the colorful lights is the answer to the riddle. All you have to do is color in the bulbs marked with an "X."

Riddle: What city has the highest electric bills in America?

© Rand McNally

N-KRA26900-R1- -1-1-1

# New Hampshire

Granite State

Capital:
Concord

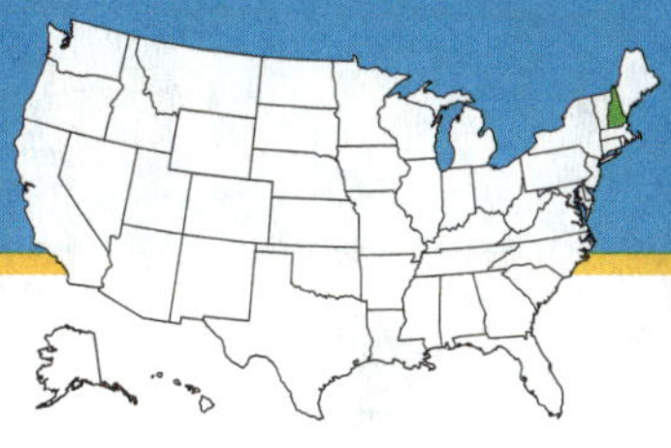

White Birch

Purple Lilac

Purple Finch

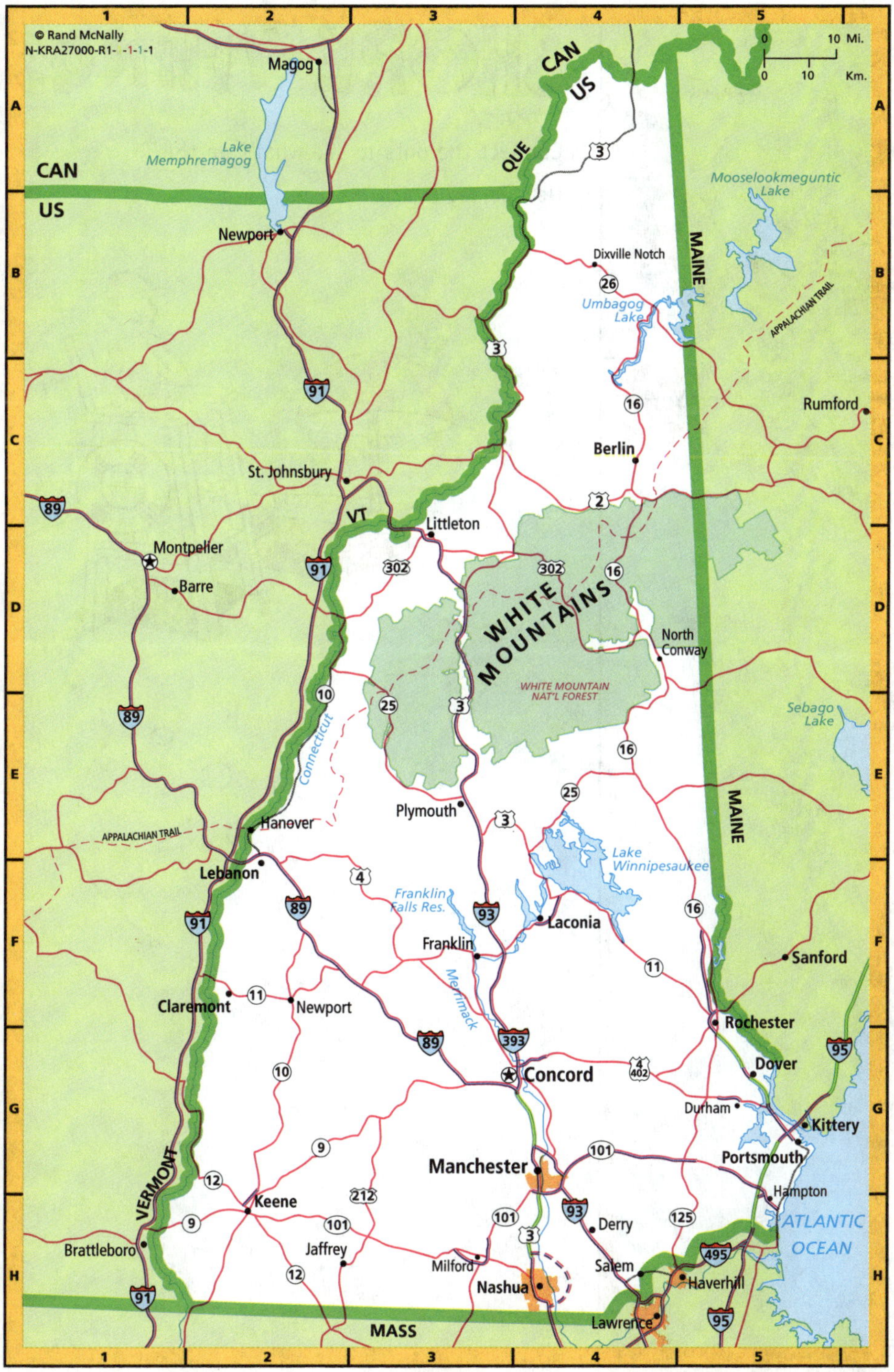

© Rand McNally
N-KRA27000-R1- -1-1-1

0 10 Mi.
0 10 Km.

CAN
US
QUE
VT
MAINE
VERMONT
MASS
Lake Memphremagog
Magog
Newport
Mooselookmeguntic Lake
Dixville Notch
Umbagog Lake
APPALACHIAN TRAIL
Rumford
Berlin
St. Johnsbury
Littleton
Montpelier
Barre
WHITE MOUNTAINS
WHITE MOUNTAIN NAT'L FOREST
North Conway
Sebago Lake
Connecticut
Plymouth
Lake Winnipesaukee
Hanover
Lebanon
Franklin Falls Res.
Laconia
Franklin
Merrimack
Sanford
Claremont
Newport
Rochester
Dover
Concord
Durham
Kittery
Portsmouth
Manchester
Hampton
Keene
Jaffrey
Derry
ATLANTIC OCEAN
Brattleboro
Milford
Salem
Haverhill
Nashua
Lawrence

## UNDER A SPELL

How many things can you find in the scene below that are spelled using one or more of the letters in NEW HAMPSHIRE?

# New Jersey

Garden State

Capital: Trenton

Red Oak

Purple Violet

Eastern Goldfinch

1 2 3 4 5

A B C D E F G H

Port Jervis
Peekskill
White Plains
Paramus
Yonkers
New Rochelle
Wayne
Paterson
Clifton
Hackensack
Passaic
Bloomfield
Newark
Irvington
Jersey City
New York
Bayonne
Elizabeth
Linden
Plainfield
Piscataway
Perth Amboy
Edison
New Brunswick
Long Beach
Sussex
Lake Hopatcong
Washington
Easton
Bethlehem
Allentown
Lehighton
Pottstown
Princeton
Trenton
Warminster
Norristown
Long Branch
Asbury Park
Lakewood
Wrightstown
Willingboro
Camden
Philadelphia
West Chester
Chester
Wilmington
Cherry Hill
Berlin
Browns Mills
Toms River
Williamstown
Hammonton
Ship Bottom
Tuckerton
Vineland
Bridgeton
Millville
Port Norris
Atlantic City
Margate City
Ocean City
Wildwood
Cape May
Dover
Milford

DELAWARE WATER GAP NATIONAL REC. AREA
ACTION PARK
NEW YORK
PENNSYLVANIA
APPALACHIAN TRAIL
NORTH EAST EXT. PENN. TURNPIKE
STATUE OF LIBERTY NAT'L MONUMENT
GATEWAY NAT'L REC. AREA
Raritan Bay
SIX FLAGS GREAT ADVENTURE
N.J. TPK.
PINE BARRENS
GARDEN ST. PKWY.
ATLANTIC CITY EXPWY.
Barnegat Bay
Great Bay
ATLANTIC OCEAN
Delaware Bay
DELAWARE
MOREY'S PIERS
PA DEL
NY CT
Hudson
PALISADES PKWY.

0 10 Mi.
0 10 Km.

© Rand McNally
N-KRA27100-R1-1-1-1-1

# SHORE THINGS

Connect the dots to see what's on this New Jersey beach.

# New Mexico

Land of Enchantment

Capital:
Santa Fe

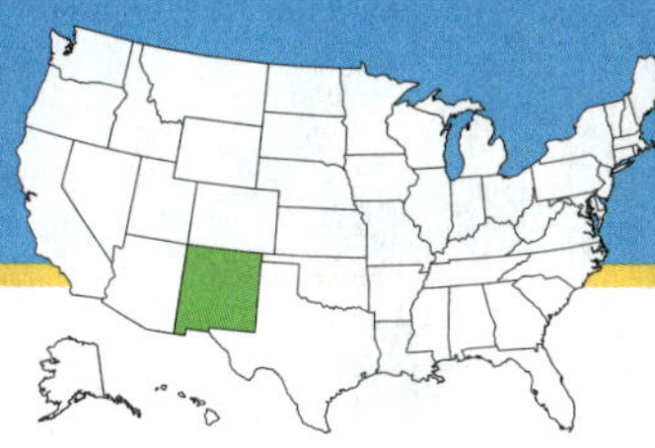

Pinon Pine

Yucca

Roadrunner

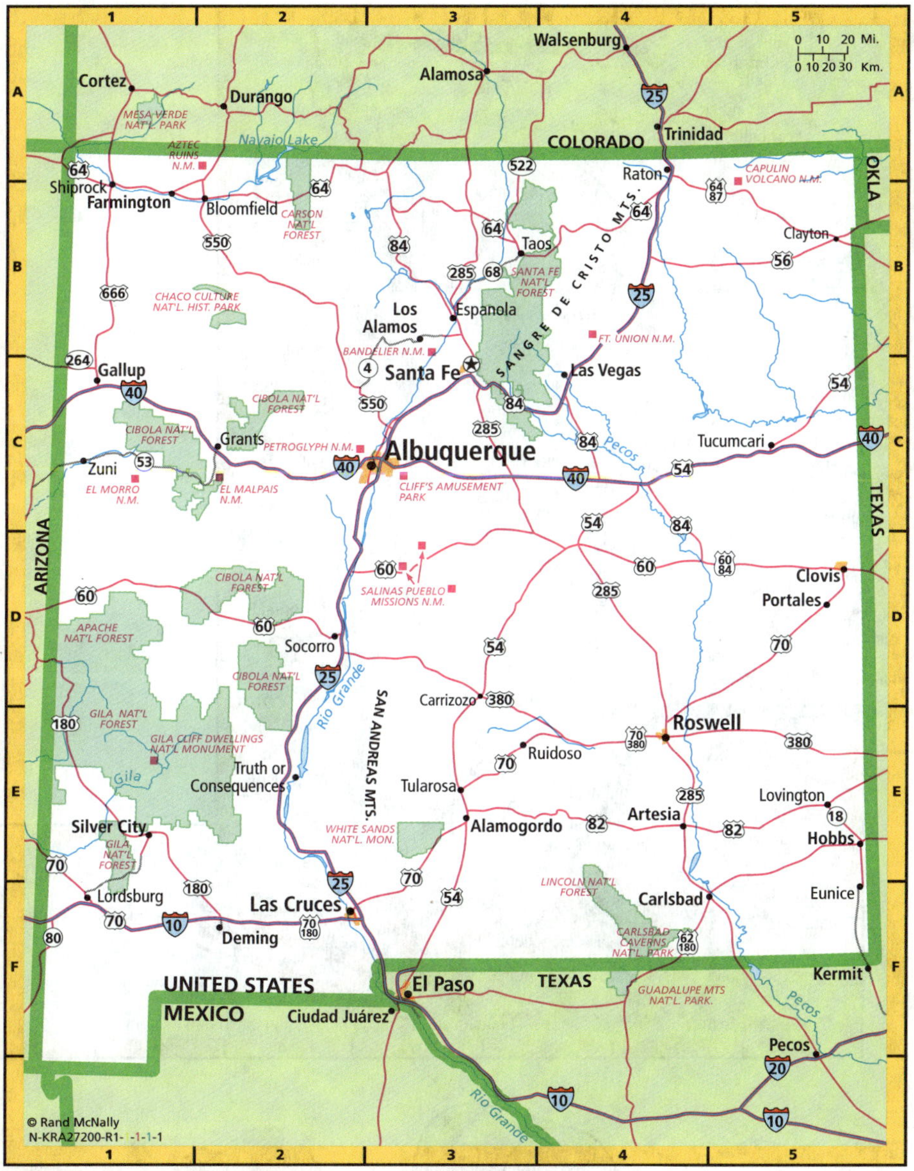

1 2 3 4 5
A B C D E F
0 10 20 Mi.
0 10 20 30 Km.
Cortez
Durango
Alamosa
Walsenburg
Trinidad
COLORADO
OKLA
MESA VERDE NAT'L PARK
AZTEC RUINS N.M.
Navajo Lake
Shiprock
Farmington
Bloomfield
CARSON NAT'L FOREST
Raton
CAPULIN VOLCANO N.M.
Clayton
Taos
SANGRE DE CRISTO MTS.
SANTA FE NAT'L FOREST
CHACO CULTURE NAT'L. HIST. PARK
Los Alamos
Espanola
BANDELIER N.M.
FT. UNION N.M.
Gallup
Santa Fe
Las Vegas
CIBOLA NAT'L FOREST
Grants
PETROGLYPH N.M.
Albuquerque
Tucumcari
Zuni
EL MORRO N.M.
EL MALPAIS N.M.
CLIFF'S AMUSEMENT PARK
Pecos
ARIZONA
TEXAS
SALINAS PUEBLO MISSIONS N.M.
Clovis
Portales
APACHE NAT'L FOREST
Socorro
Rio Grande
SAN ANDREAS MTS.
Carrizozo
Roswell
GILA NAT'L FOREST
GILA CLIFF DWELLINGS NAT'L MONUMENT
Gila
Truth or Consequences
Ruidoso
Tularosa
Lovington
Artesia
Hobbs
Silver City
WHITE SANDS NAT'L. MON.
Alamogordo
LINCOLN NAT'L FOREST
Eunice
Lordsburg
Las Cruces
Carlsbad
Deming
CARLSBAD CAVERNS NAT'L. PARK
UNITED STATES
MEXICO
El Paso
TEXAS
Kermit
GUADALUPE MTS NAT'L. PARK.
Ciudad Juárez
Pecos
© Rand McNally
N-KRA27200-R1- -1-1-1

# HOT TIME!

The Hot Air Balloon Festival in Albuquerque is the most photographed event of its kind in the world! New Mexico is famous for another hot thing—its southwestern food. Can you find the 10 chili peppers hiding in this scene?

# New York

Empire State

Capital:
Albany

Sugar Maple

Rose

Red-Breasted Bluebird

# PROBLEMS AT THE PARK

The state of New York has many beautiful parks,
but there seems to be something strange going on in this one.
Can you spot 10 things wrong in the park?

# North Carolina

Tar Heel State

Capital: Raleigh

Long Leaf Pine

Dogwood

Cardinal

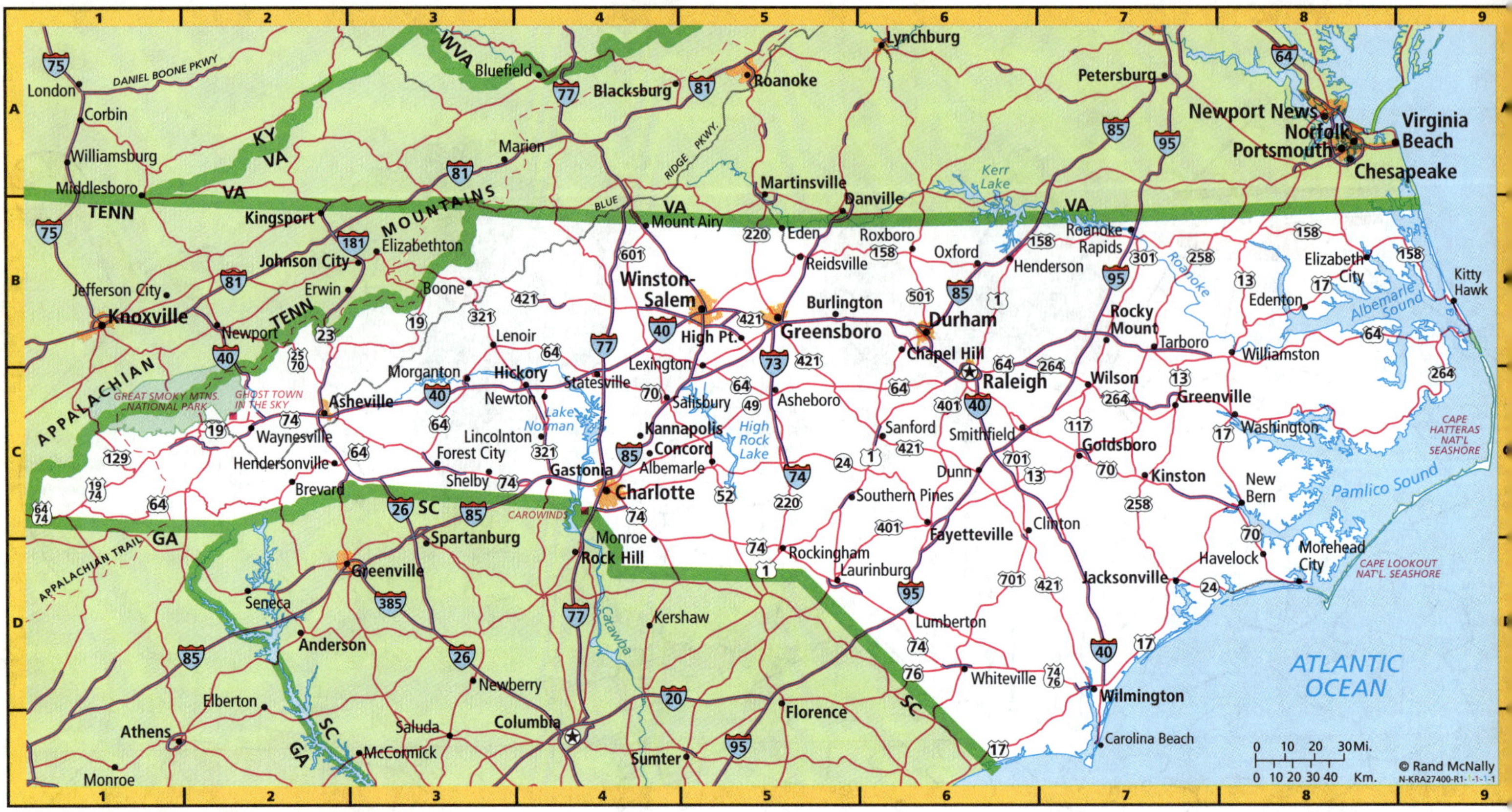

## First in Flight

The beach community of Kitty Hawk (B-9) was the site of the Wright brothers' first airplane flight. Try to find all the things that start with "F" in this beach scene.

# North Dakota

Peace Garden State

Capital: Bismarck

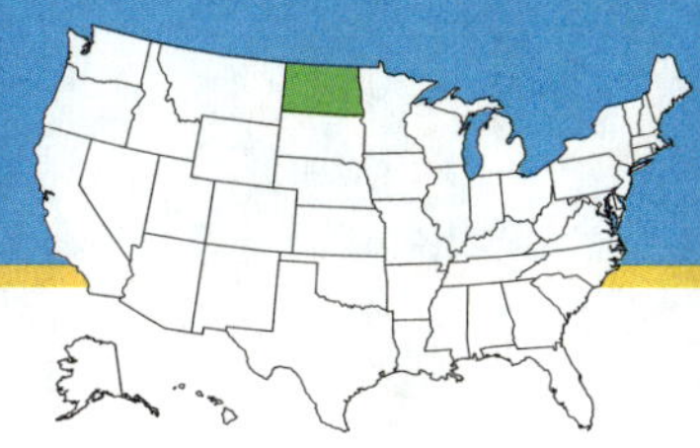

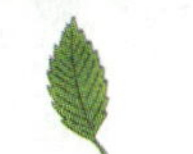

American Elm

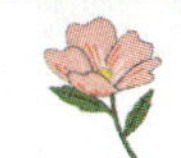

Wild Prairie Rose

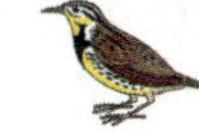

Western Meadowlark

# Secret Cities

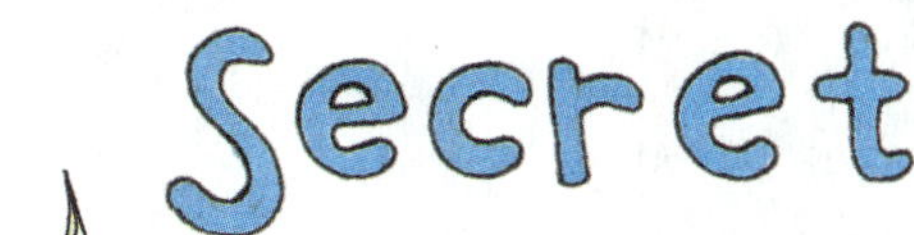

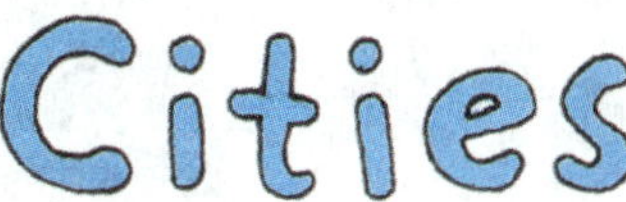

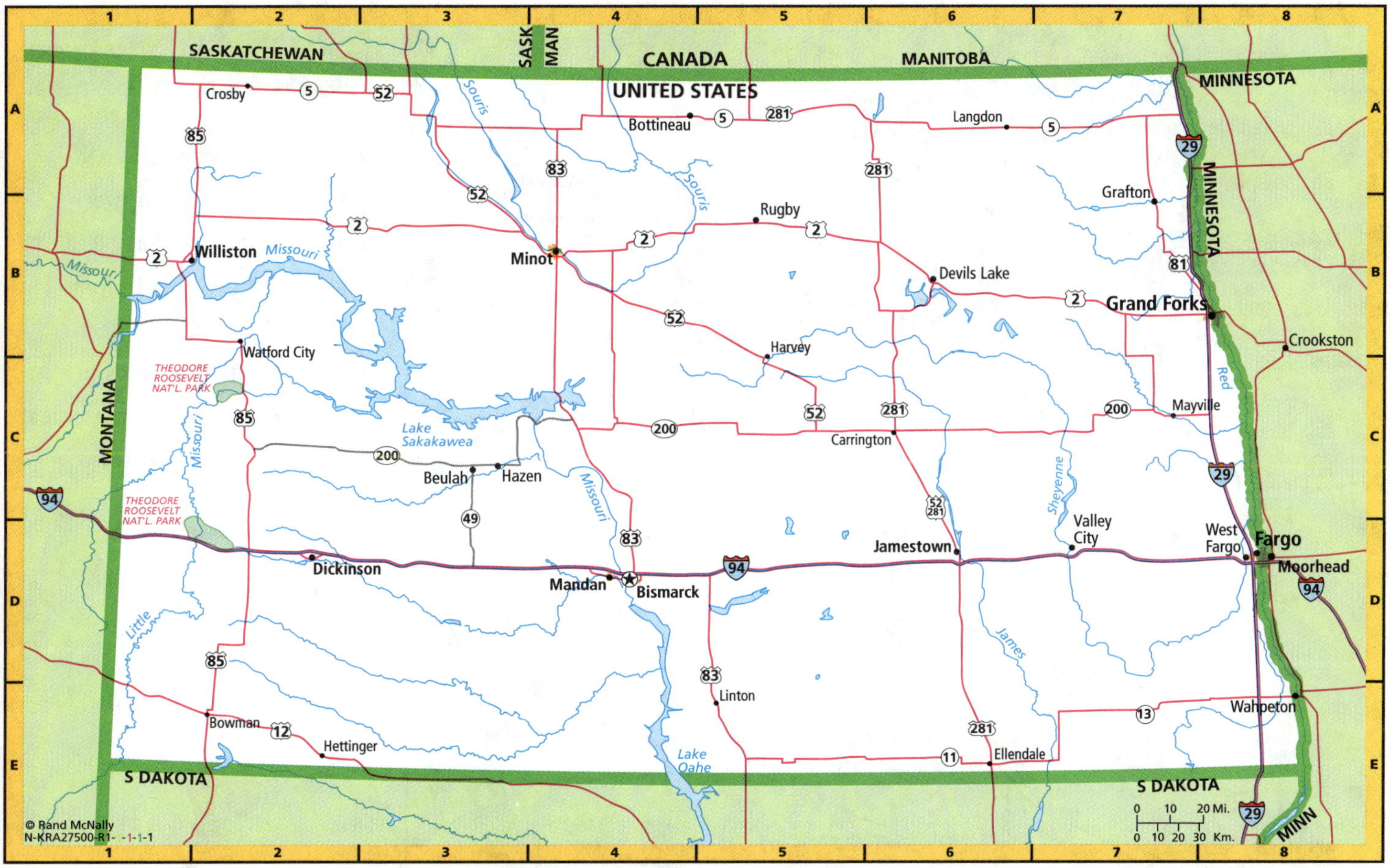

Figure out the names of 6 North Dakota cities using the word puzzles below.

① 

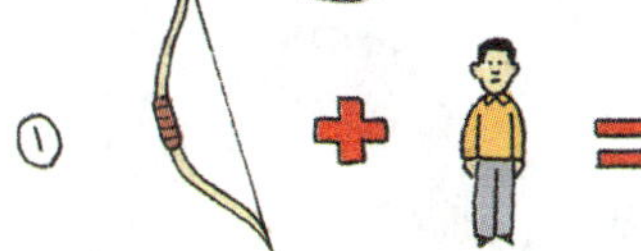

② 

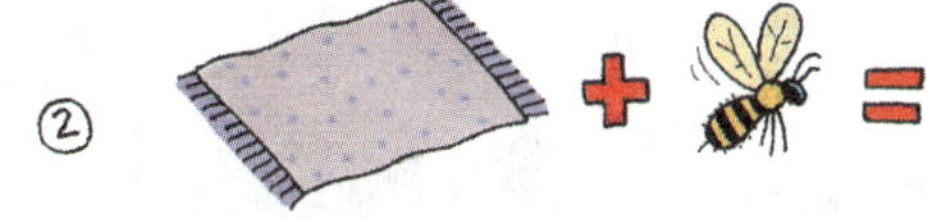

③ 


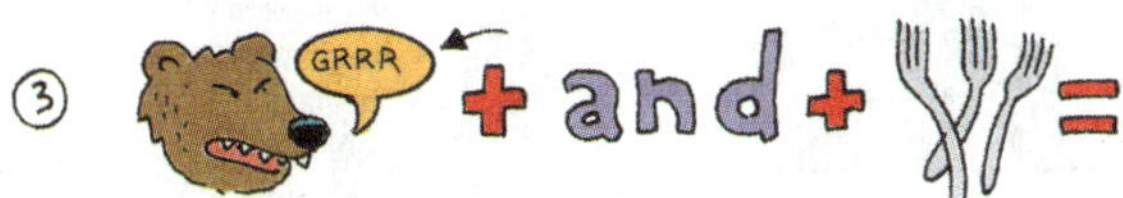

④ 


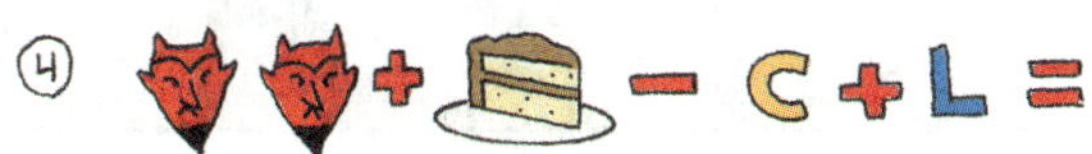

⑤ 


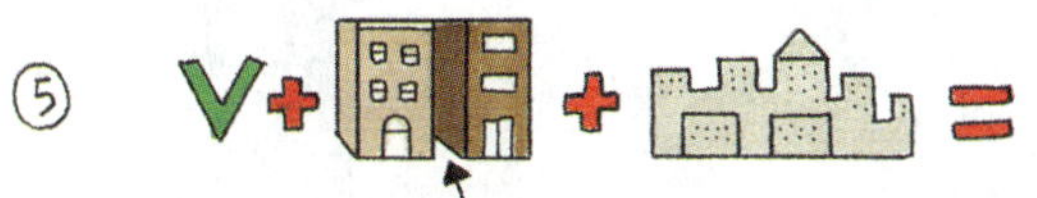

⑥

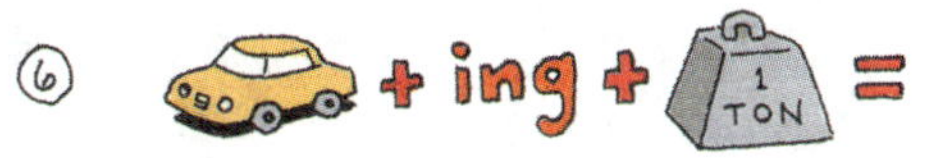

Buckeye State

Capital: Columbus

Buckeye

Scarlet Carnation

Cardinal

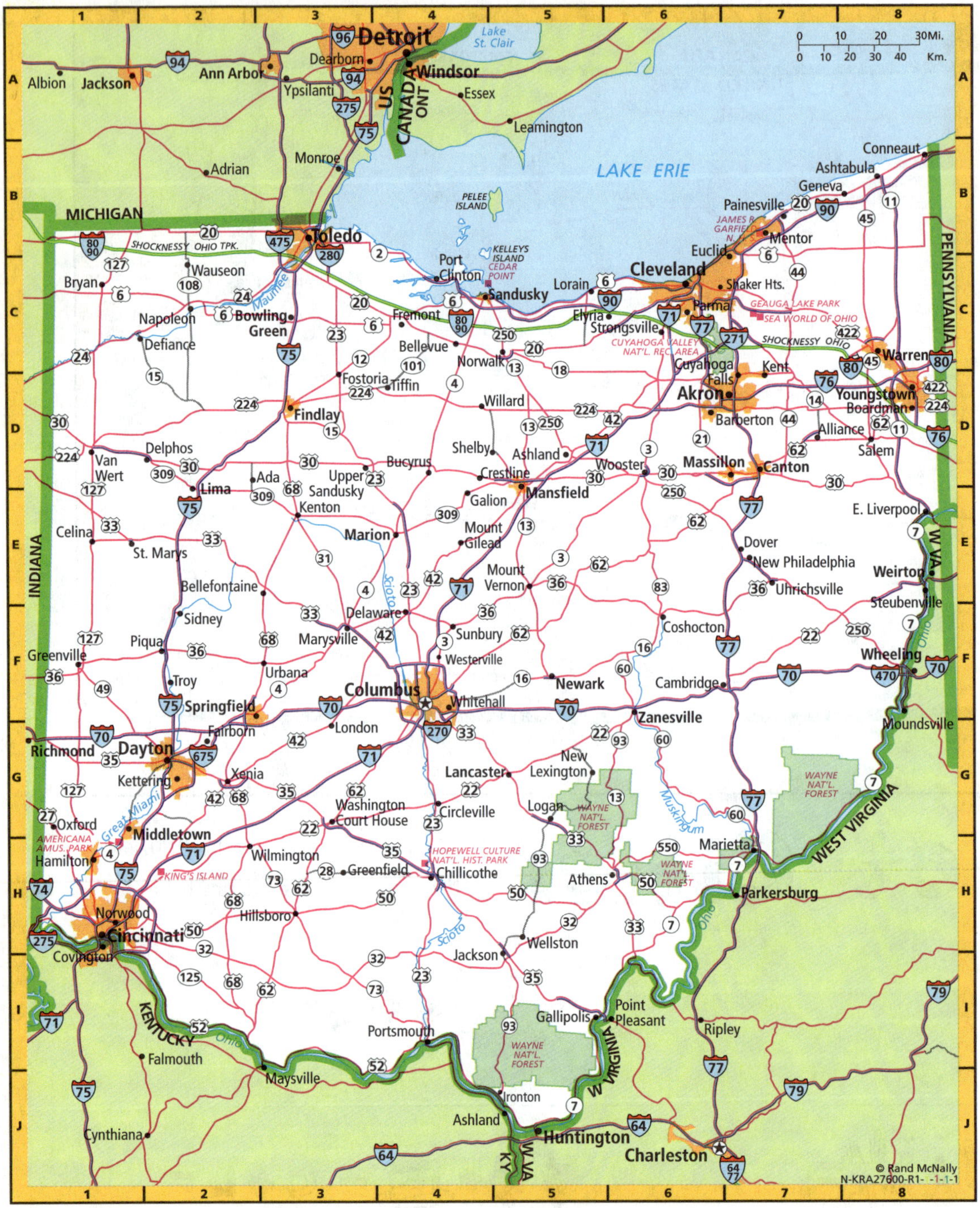

The names of many cities in Ohio can be split into two smaller words. For example, DAY and TON go together to form DAYTON. Match the words in column A with the words in column B to spell 12 Ohio cities. All of the cities are listed on the map.

© Rand McNally
N-KRA27600-R1- -1-1-1

| Column A | Column B |
|---|---|
| FIND | LAND |
| NEW | MOUTH |
| ASH | FIELD |
| CAN | TOWN |
| WHITE | ARK |
| SPRING | TON |
| LOG | BORN |
| AT | AN |
| PORTS | FORD |
| OX | LAY |
| FAIR | HALL |
| MIDDLE | HENS |

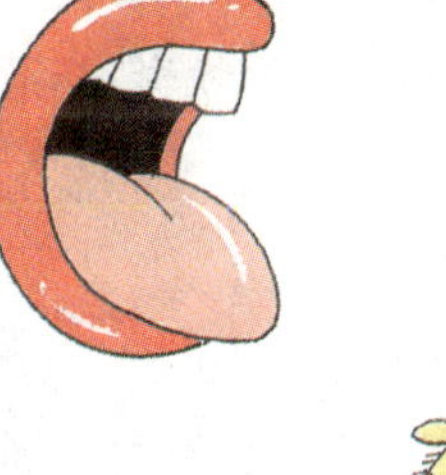

# Oklahoma

Sooner State

Capital: Oklahoma City

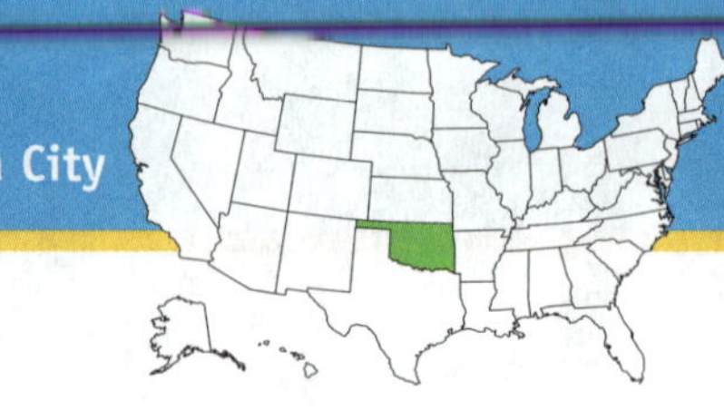

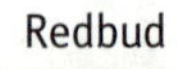

Redbud

Mistletoe

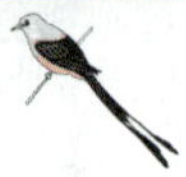

Scissor-tailed Flycatcher

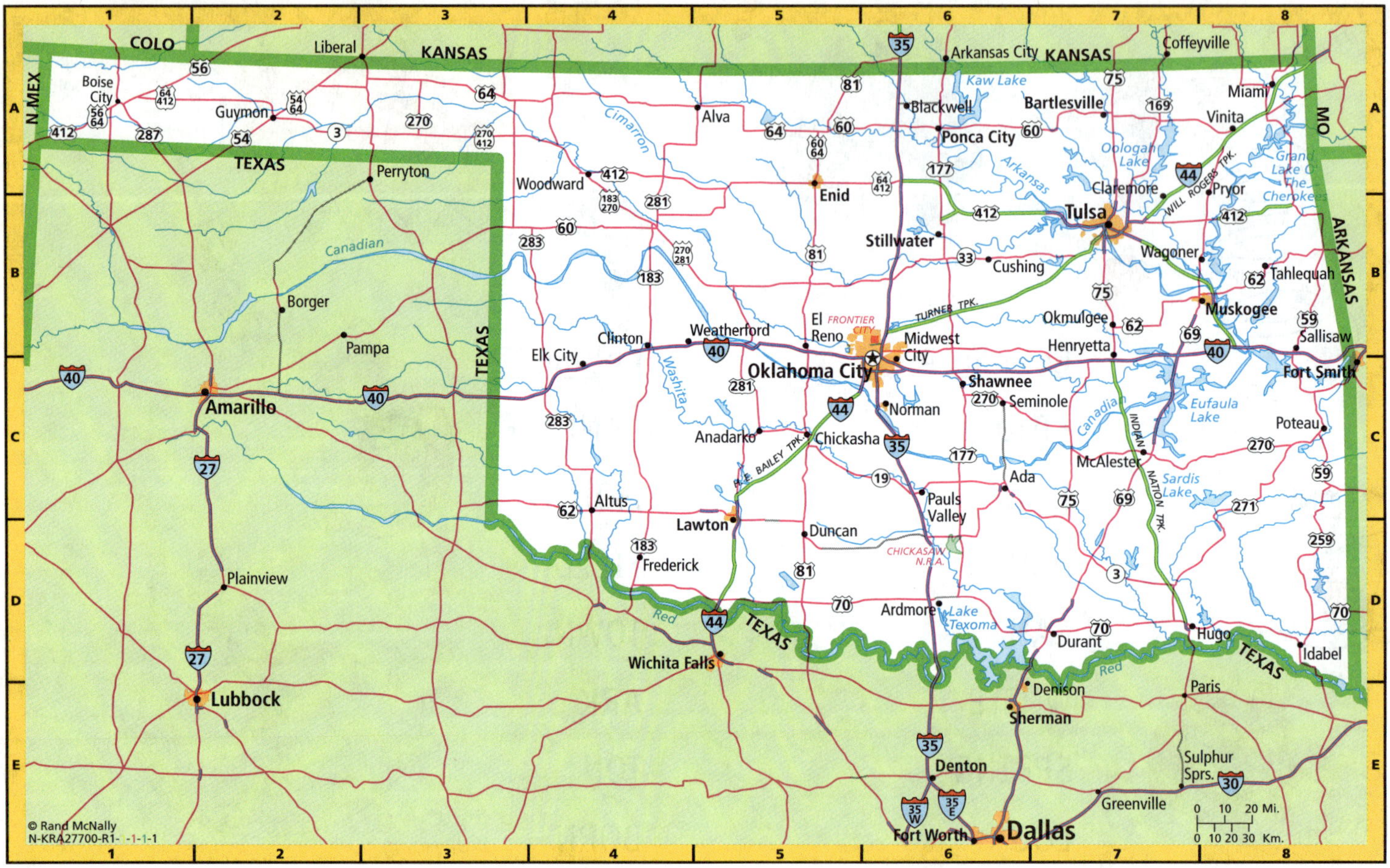

COLO
KANSAS
N MEX
TEXAS
MO
ARKANSAS
Boise City
Guymon
Liberal
Perryton
Borger
Pampa
Amarillo
Plainview
Lubbock
Woodward
Alva
Enid
Arkansas City
Coffeyville
Blackwell
Ponca City
Bartlesville
Miami
Vinita
Claremore
Pryor
Tulsa
Stillwater
Cushing
Wagoner
Tahlequah
Muskogee
Okmulgee
Henryetta
Sallisaw
Fort Smith
Elk City
Clinton
Weatherford
El Reno
Frontier City
Midwest City
Oklahoma City
Shawnee
Seminole
Norman
Anadarko
Chickasha
McAlester
Poteau
Ada
Pauls Valley
Altus
Lawton
Duncan
Frederick
Chickasaw N.R.A.
Ardmore
Lake Texoma
Durant
Hugo
Idabel
Wichita Falls
Denison
Sherman
Paris
Denton
Sulphur Sprs.
Greenville
Fort Worth
Dallas
Canadian
Cimarron
Arkansas
Washita
Red
Kaw Lake
Oologah Lake
Grand Lake O' The Cherokees
Eufaula Lake
Sardis Lake
Turner Tpk.
Will Rogers Tpk.
Indian Nation Tpk.
H.E. Bailey Tpk.

© Rand McNally
N-KRA27700-R1- -1-1-1

# Scrambled Cities

Unscramble the names of these Oklahoma towns and you'll be OK!

DINE (A-5) ______

BILEAD (D-8) ______

LOWTAN (C-5) ______

WASSAIL (B-8) ______

LEEKOMUG (B-7) ______

MOUNGY (A-2) ______

USALT (B-7) ______

AMIMI (A-8) ______

SHEENWA (C-6) ______

TALLIWERTS (B-6) ______

# OREGON

Beaver State

Capital: Salem

Douglas Fir

Oregon Grape

Western Meadowlark

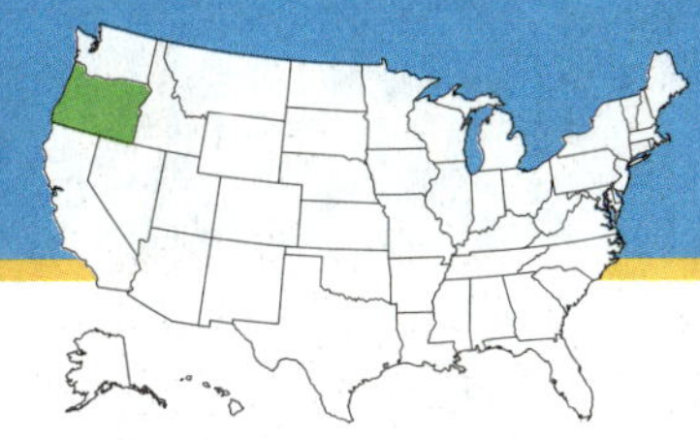

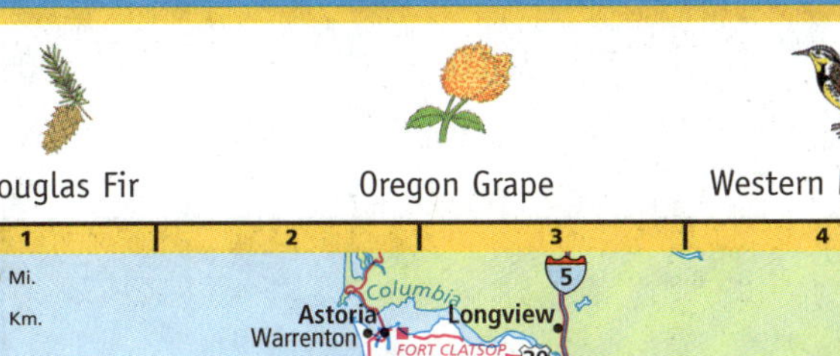

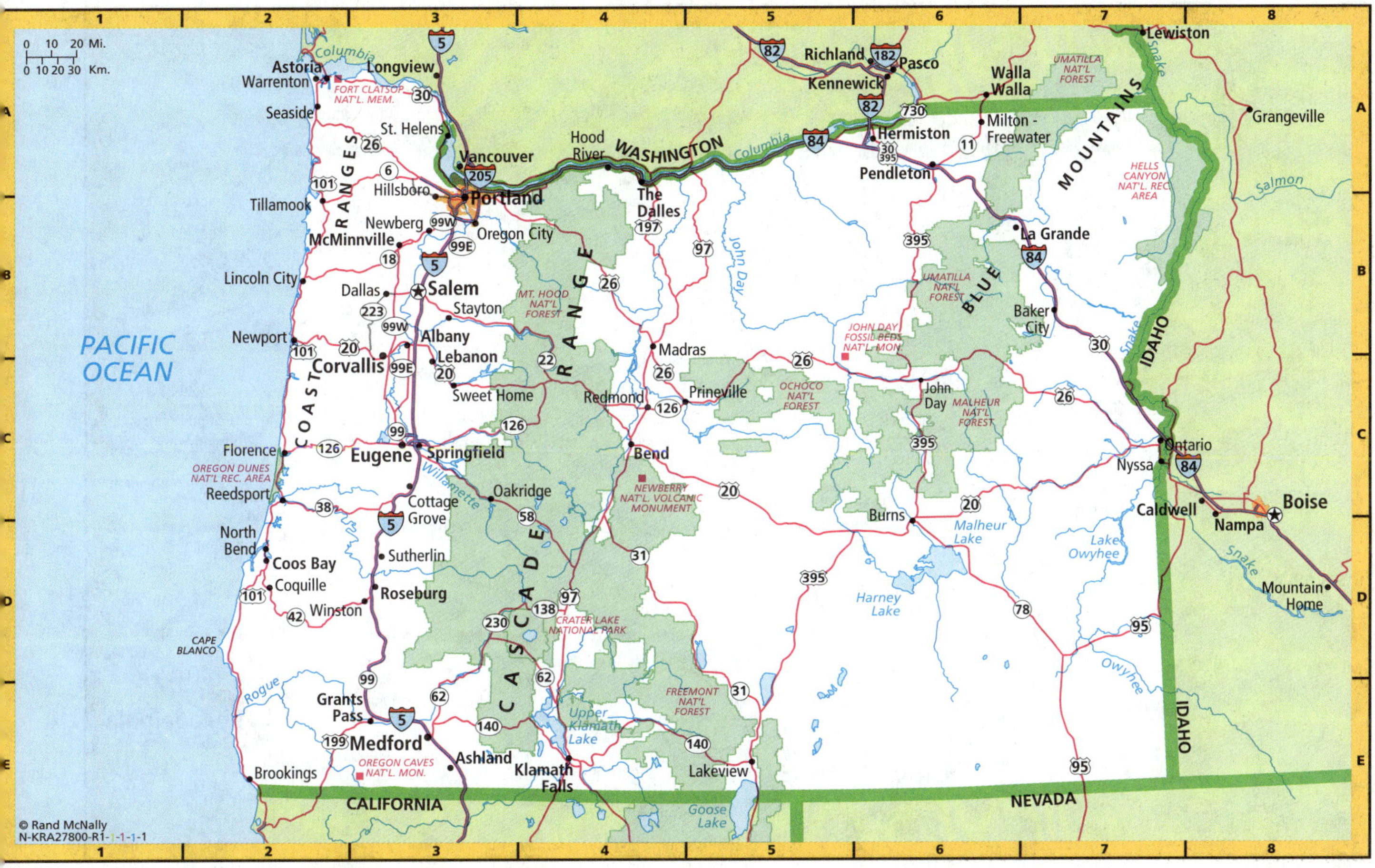

## DIVE IN

These two tide pools on the Oregon coast are almost exactly alike. Can you spot the differences between them?

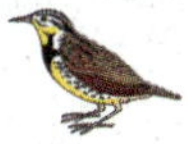

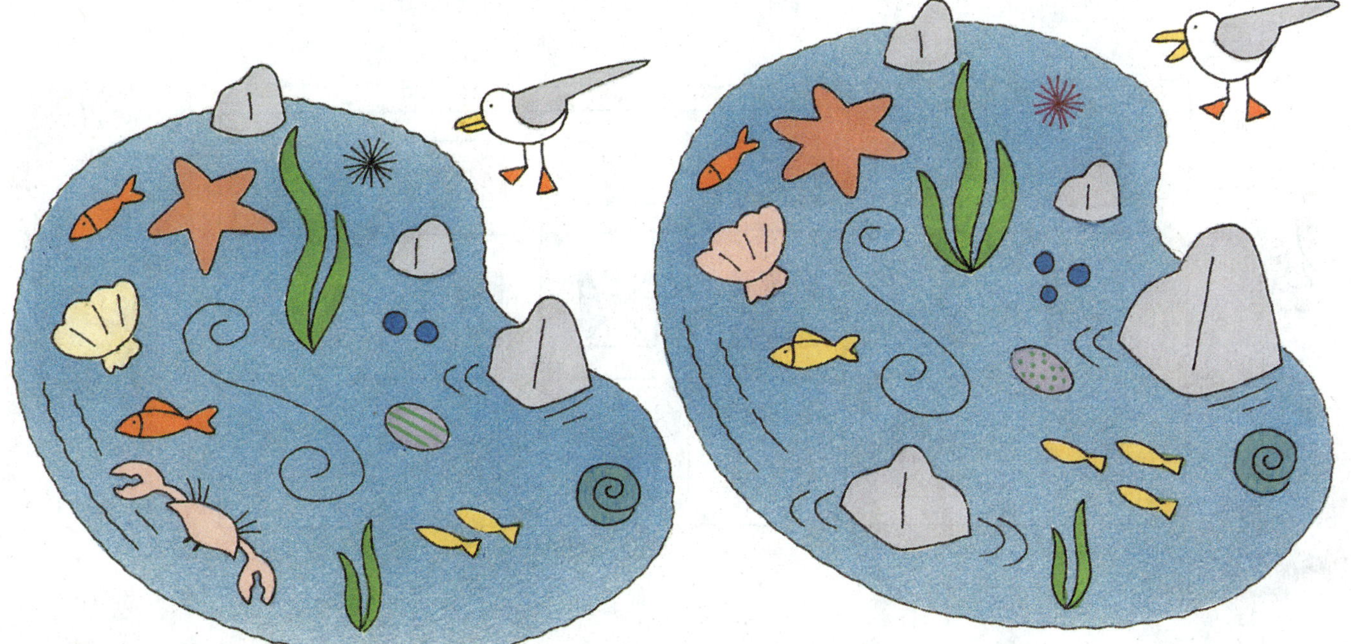

# Pennsylvania

Keystone State

Capital: Harrisburg

Hemlock

Mountain Laurel

Ruffed Grouse

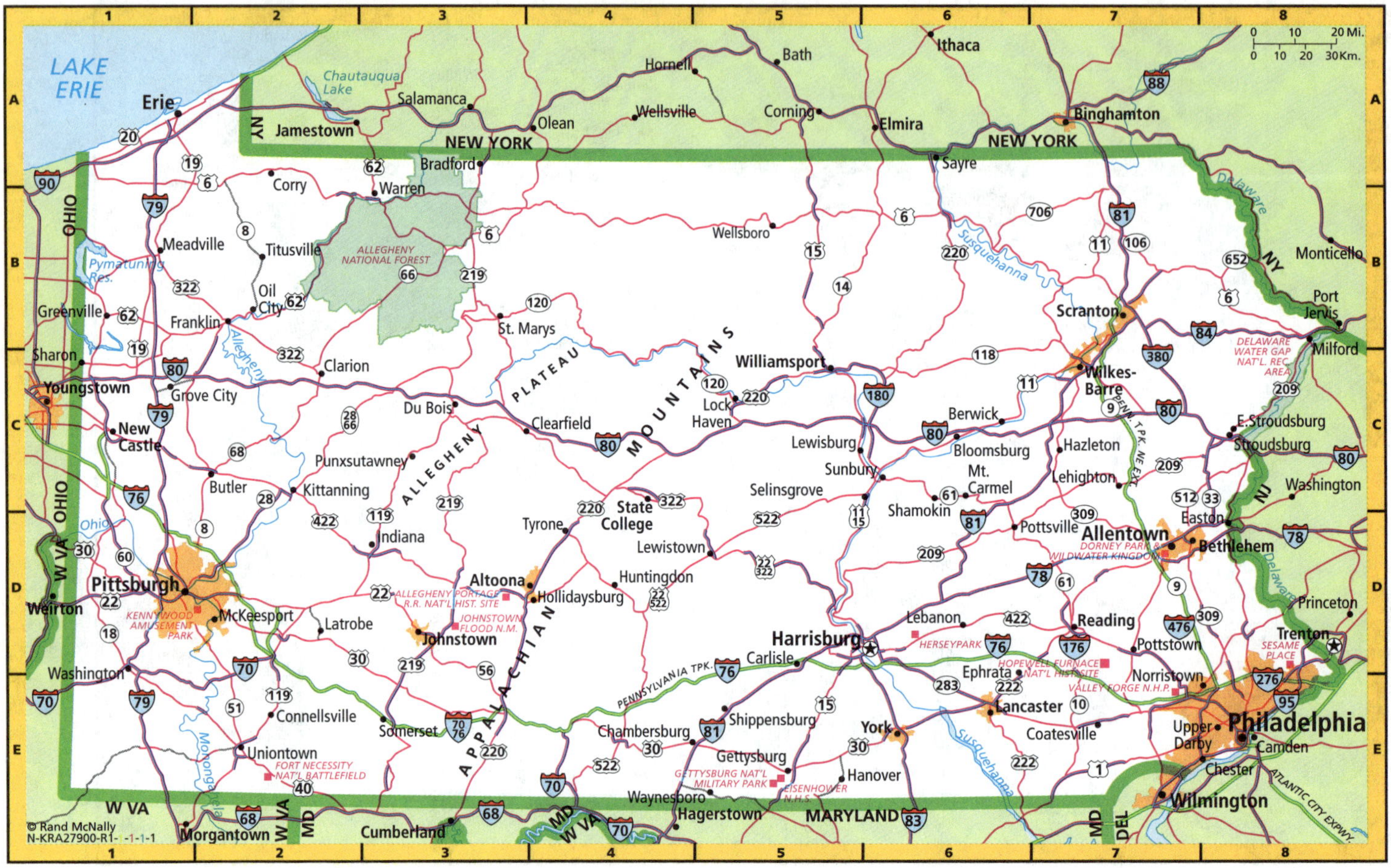

LAKE ERIE
Erie
Jamestown
Chautauqua Lake
Salamanca
Olean
Bradford
Hornell
Wellsville
Bath
Corning
Ithaca
Elmira
Binghamton
Sayre
NEW YORK
Warren
Corry
Meadville
Titusville
ALLEGHENY NATIONAL FOREST
Pymatuning Res.
Oil City
Franklin
Greenville
Sharon
Youngstown
Grove City
Clarion
New Castle
Butler
Kittanning
Punxsutawney
Du Bois
St. Marys
Clearfield
ALLEGHENY PLATEAU
ALLEGHENY MOUNTAINS
Wellsboro
Williamsport
Lock Haven
Lewisburg
Sunbury
Selinsgrove
Shamokin
Mt. Carmel
Berwick
Bloomsburg
Hazleton
Scranton
Wilkes-Barre
Lehighton
Pottsville
Allentown
Bethlehem
Easton
DORNEY PARK & WILDWATER KINGDOM
E. Stroudsburg
Stroudsburg
Monticello
Port Jervis
Milford
DELAWARE WATER GAP NAT'L. REC. AREA
Washington
Princeton
Trenton
SESAME PLACE
Pittsburgh
Weirton
KENNYWOOD AMUSEMENT PARK
McKeesport
Washington
Latrobe
Indiana
Johnstown
JOHNSTOWN FLOOD N.M.
ALLEGHENY PORTAGE R.R. NAT'L HIST. SITE
Altoona
Hollidaysburg
Tyrone
State College
Huntingdon
Lewistown
APPALACHIAN MOUNTAINS
Harrisburg
Carlisle
PENNSYLVANIA TPK.
Lebanon
HERSEYPARK
Reading
Pottstown
Norristown
Ephrata
HOPEWELL FURNACE NAT'L HIST. SITE
VALLEY FORGE N.H.P.
Lancaster
Coatesville
Philadelphia
Camden
Upper Darby
Chester
Wilmington
ATLANTIC CITY EXPWY.
York
Hanover
Gettysburg
GETTYSBURG NAT'L MILITARY PARK
EISENHOWER N.H.S.
Shippensburg
Chambersburg
Waynesboro
Hagerstown
MARYLAND
Connellsville
Somerset
Uniontown
FORT NECESSITY NAT'L BATTLEFIELD
Morgantown
Cumberland
OHIO
W VA
MD
NJ
NY
DEL
Susquehanna
Delaware
Allegheny
Monongahela
Ohio
0 10 20 Mi.
0 10 20 30 Km.

## Two of a kind

Two of these squares in the Pennsylvania Dutch quilt are exactly the same. Can you find them?

# Rhode Island

Ocean State

Capital: Providence

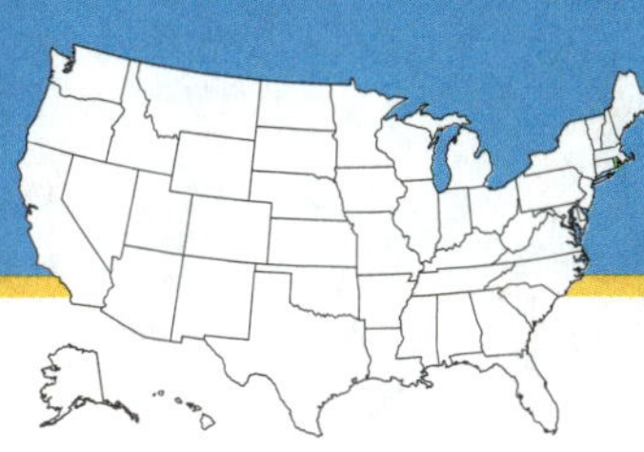

Red Maple

Violet

Rhode Island Red

People in Rhode Island must like the color red. Their state bird is the Rhode Island Red and their state tree is the Red Maple. Can you identify the words and phrases below that contain the word RED?

1. Stop signal ______________________________

2. Tall California tree ______________________________

3. Colors of the U.S. flag ______________________________

4. Become very angry ______________________________

5. Story about a girl, her grandmother, and a wolf ______________________________

______________________________

6. Walking surface for VIPs ______________________________

7. Carrot top ______________________________

# South Carolina

Palmetto State

Capital: Columbia

Palmetto

Carolina Jessamine

Carolina Wren

1 2 3 4 5 6 7

A B C D E F

N CAR
GA
NORTH CAROLINA
GA
GEORGIA
Gastonia
Charlotte
COWPENS NAT'L. BATTLEFIELD
KINGS MTN. NAT'L. MIL. PARK
Gaffney
York
Spartanburg
Rock Hill
Fayetteville
Lake Keowee
SUMTER N. F.
Seneca
Clemson
Greenville
Union
Chester
Lancaster
Cheraw
Bennettsville
Anderson
Laurens
Clinton
SUMTER NATIONAL FOREST
Hartsville
Dillon
Hartwell Lake
Abbeville
Greenwood
Newberry
Camden
Darlington
Florence
Marion
Elberton
NINETY SIX NAT'L. HIST. SITE
Lake Murray
Columbia
Athens
SUMTER NATIONAL FOREST
J. Strom Thurmond Lake
Sumter
Lake City
CONGAREE SWAMP NAT'L. MON.
Lake Marion
Myrtle Beach
MYRTLE BEACH PAVILION AND AMUS. PARK
Aiken
Thomson
Augusta
Orangeburg
Georgetown
Barnwell
Lake Moultrie
Santee
FRANCIS MARION NATIONAL FOREST
Waynesboro
Walterboro
N. Charleston
Charleston
FT. SUMTER NAT'L. MON.
Folly Beach
Savannah
Swainsboro
Beaufort
Edisto Beach
ATLANTIC OCEAN
Eastman
Hilton Head Island
Savannah
0 10 20 30 Mi.
0 10 20 30 40 Km.

Cotton is an important crop in South Carolina. Can you find the pesky boll weevils hidden in the cotton plants? Cross them out before they damage the cotton.

# South Dakota

Mount Rushmore State

Capital: Pierre

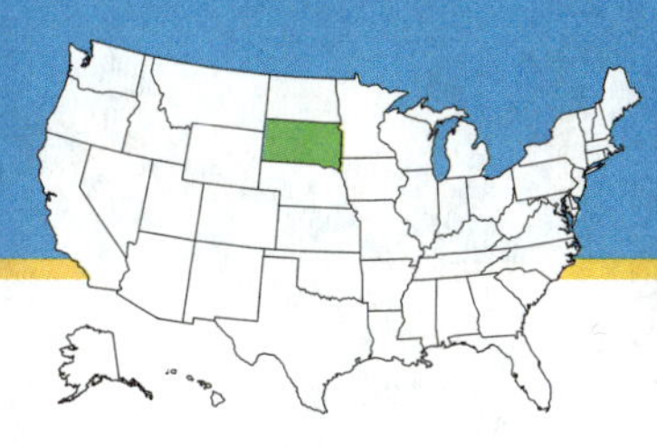

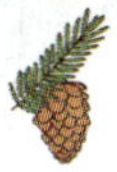

Black Hills Spruce

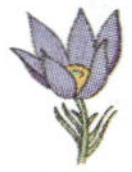

Pasque Flower

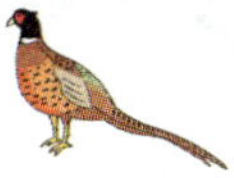

Chinese Ring-necked Pheasant

# Wild AND WOOLY

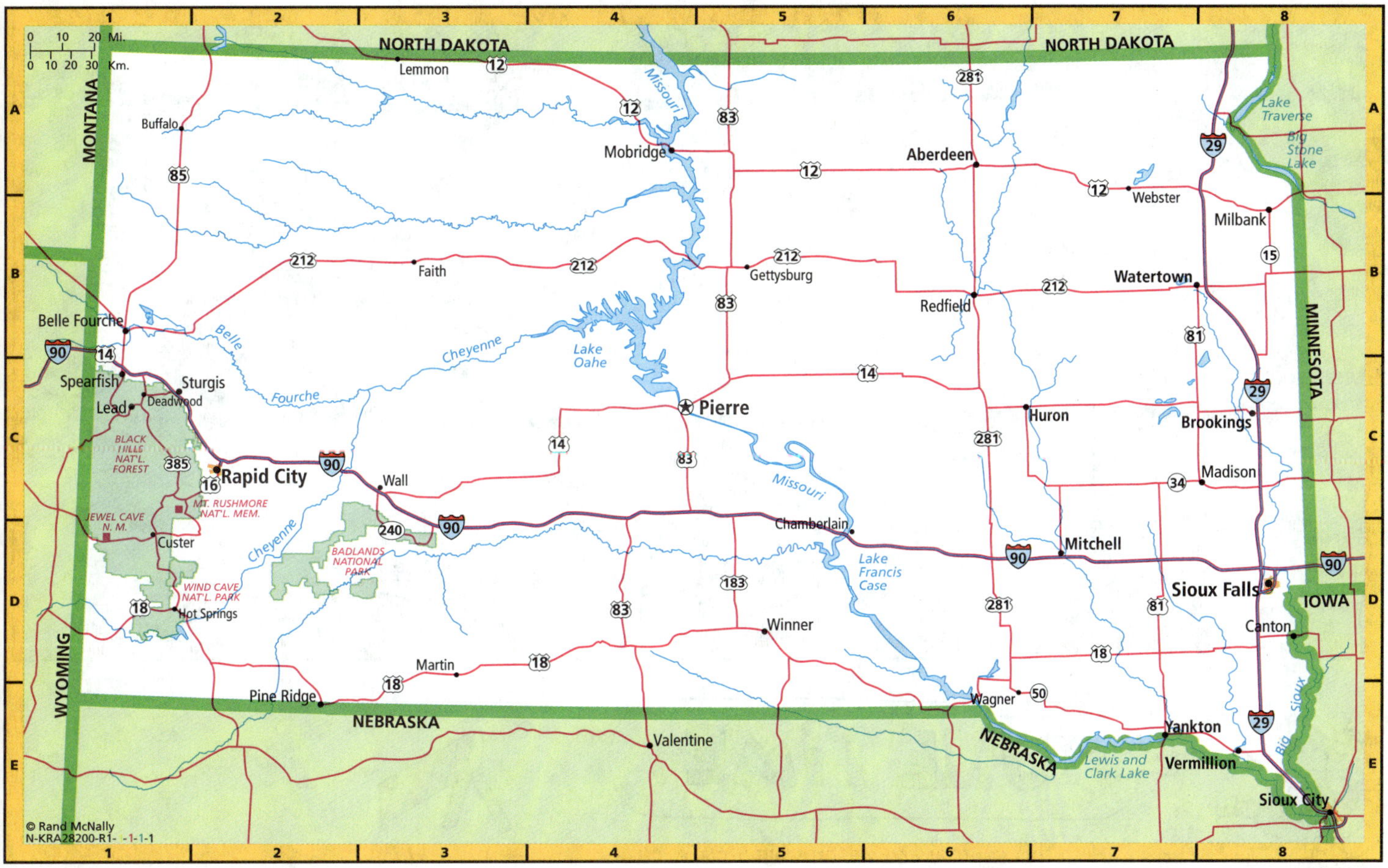

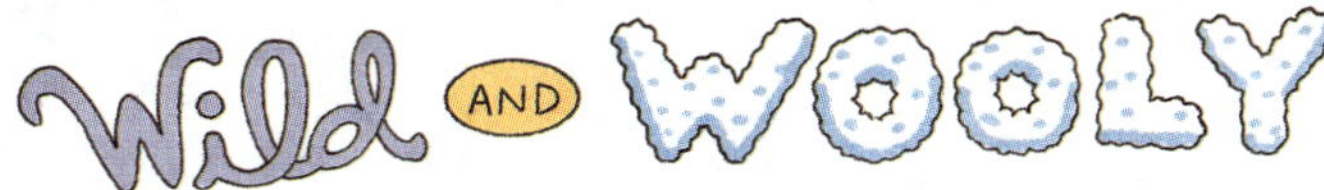

The pictures below show the steps in making a sweater—starting with shearing a sheep for wool. However, the pictures are not in the right order. If you write the letters in the corner of the pictures in the order in which they should be placed, the letters will complete a fact about South Dakota.

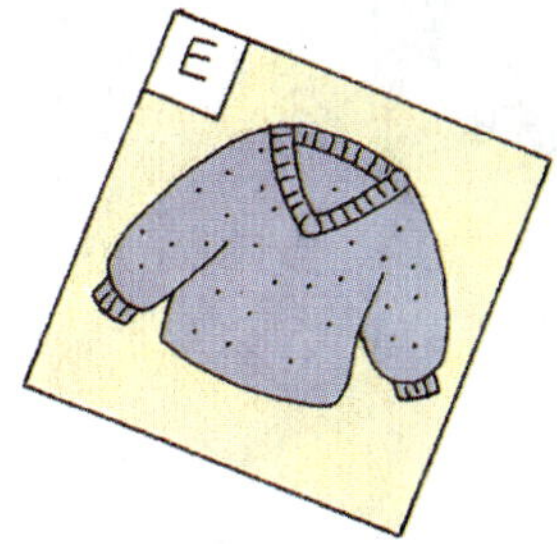

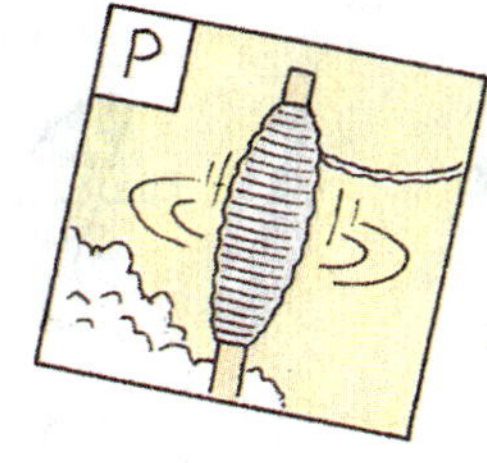

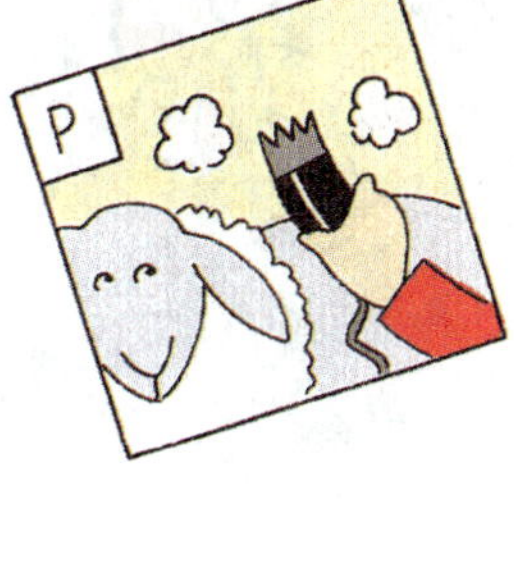

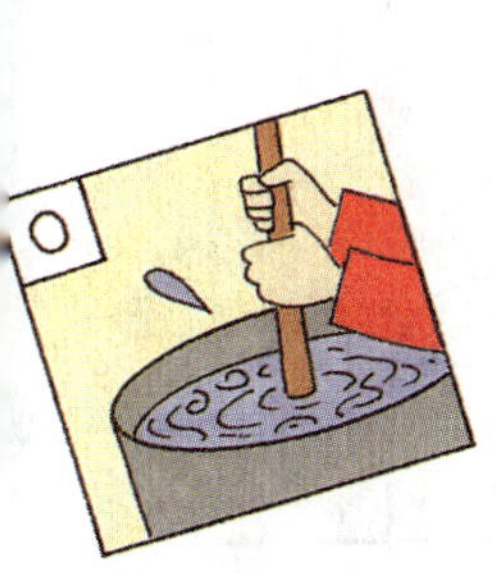

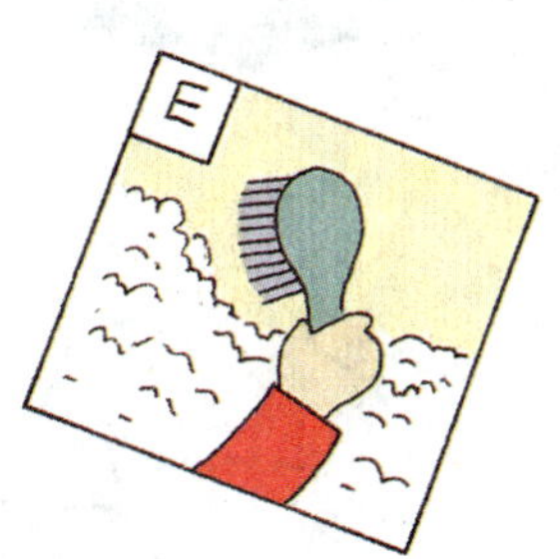

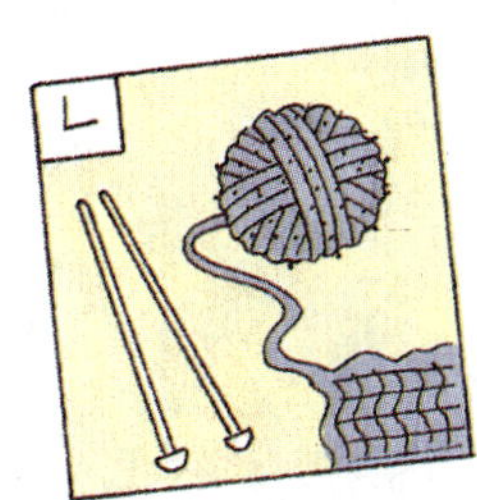

In South Dakota, there are twice as many sheep as ______ ______ ______ ______ ______ ______.

# Tennessee

Volunteer State

Capital:
Nashville

Tulip Poplar

Iris

Mockingbird

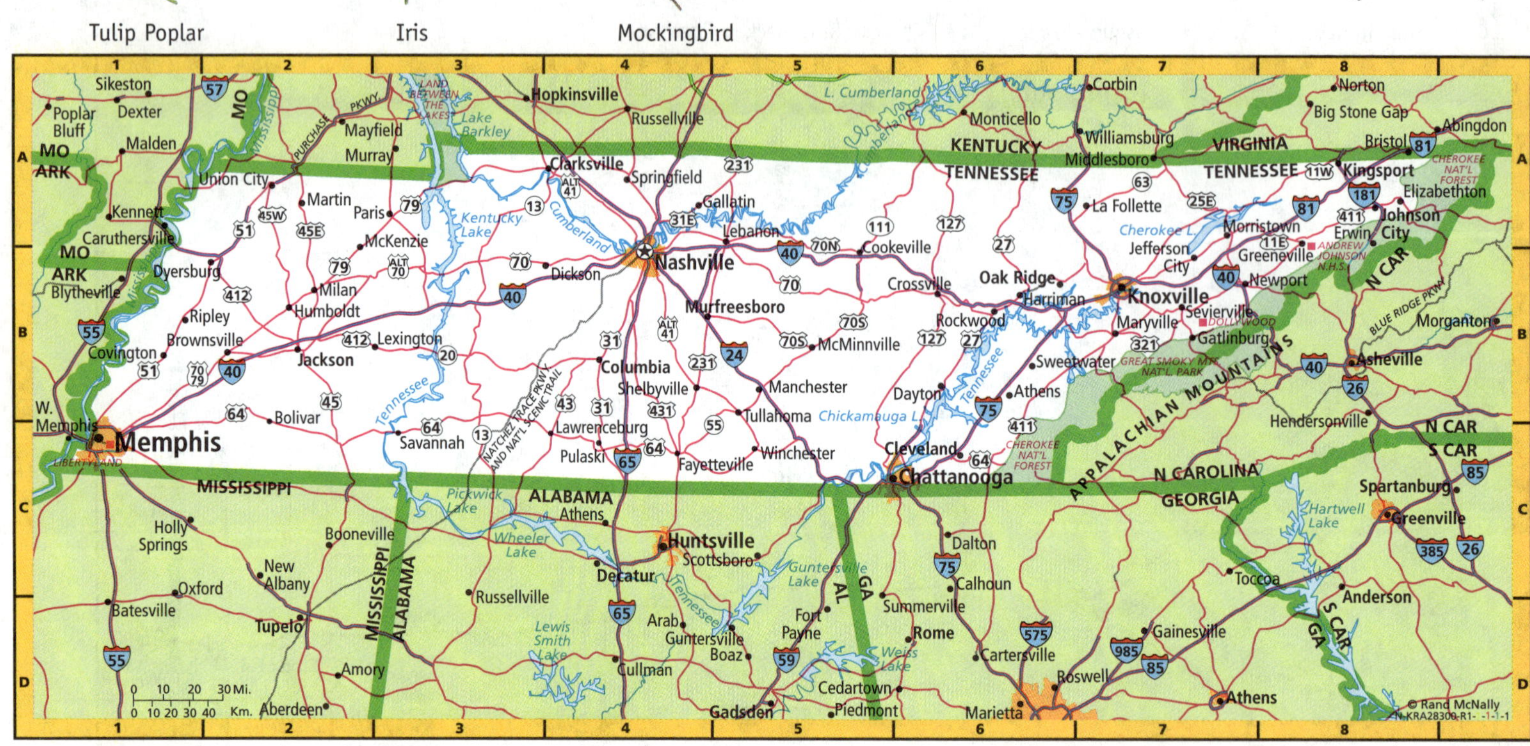

## TUNE TIME

Help this country and western band make it to the Grand Ole Opry in time.

ROAD CLOSED
STOP
GRAND OLE OPRY

# TeXas

Lone Star State

Capital:
Austin

Pecan

Bluebonnet

Mockingbird

OKLAHOMA · NEW MEXICO · MEXICO · CHIHUAHUA · COAHUILA · NUEVO LEON · TAMAULIPAS · OKLA · ARK · LA · MEX · UNITED STATES · GULF OF MEXICO · EDWARDS PLATEAU

0 10 20 30 40 Mi.
0 20 40 60 Km.

Perryton, Dalhart, Dumas, Borger, Pampa, Amarillo, Canyon, Hereford, Clovis, Portales, Plainview, Littlefield, Lubbock, Levelland, Brownfield, Roswell, Ruidoso, Alamogordo, Artesia, Lovington, Hobbs, Seminole, Lamesa, Snyder, Sweetwater, Las Cruces, Carlsbad, Andrews, El Paso, Ciudad Juarez, Fabens, Kermit, Odessa, Midland, Big Spring, Monahans, Pecos, Childress, Vernon, Lawton, Duncan, Wichita Falls, Ardmore, Durant, Hugo, Idabel, Hope, Texarkana, Gainesville, Sherman, Denison, Paris, Denton, Commerce, Greenville, Sulphur Springs, Mt. Pleasant, Atlanta, Mineral Wells, Breckenridge, Ft. Worth, Weatherford, Arlington, Dallas, Terrell, Marshall, Shreveport, Abilene, Stephenville, Ennis, Corsicana, Tyler, Kilgore, Longview, Carthage, Athens, Henderson, Mansfield, Hillsboro, Coleman, Brownwood, San Angelo, Mexia, Palestine, Nacogdoches, Gatesville, Waco, Crockett, Lufkin, Killeen, Temple, Cameron, Brady, Lampasas, Georgetown, Bryan, Huntsville, Livingston, Jasper, Navasota, Conroe, Beaumont, Orange, Fredericksburg, Austin, Brenham, Houston, Port Arthur, Baytown, Kerrville, San Marcos, Lockhart, New Braunfels, Seguin, Gonzales, San Antonio, Hondo, Uvalde, Wharton, Texas City, Galveston, Freeport, El Campo, Bay City, Cuero, Victoria, Pleasanton, Pearsall, Crystal City, Eagle Pass, Piedras Negras, Del Rio, Port Lavaca, Beeville, Sinton, Aransas Pass, Corpus Christi, Mathis, Alice, Kingsville, Laredo, Nuevo Laredo, Falfurrias, Zapata, Rio Grande City, Edinburg, McAllen, Raymondville, Harlingen, Reynosa, Brownsville, Matamoros, Monterrey, Saltillo, Sabinas Hidalgo, Monclova, Nueva Rosita, Sabinas, Chihuahua, Villa Ahumada, Presidio, Alpine, Fort Stockton

Canadian, Red, Pecos, Colorado, Rio Grande, Conchos, Sabine, Lake Texoma, Toledo Bend Res.

LAKE MEREDITH N.R.A., JOYLAND AMUSEMENT PARK, WHITE SANDS NAT'L MON., CARLSBAD CAVERNS NAT'L PARK, GUADALUPE MOUNTAINS NAT'L PARK, SIX FLAGS OVER TEXAS, DAVY CROCKETT NAT'L FOREST, SAM HOUSTON NAT'L FOREST, SIX FLAGS ASTROWORLD / WATERWORLD, AMISTAD NAT'L REC. AREA, SIX FLAGS FIESTA TEXAS, SEA WORLD OF TEXAS, BIG BEND NAT'L PARK, PADRE ISLAND NATIONAL SEASHORE

IN PLANE SIGHT

Can you find the people below in the Dallas/Fort Worth airport scene?

# Utah

Beehive State

Capital:
Salt Lake City

Blue Spruce

Sego Lily

American Seagull

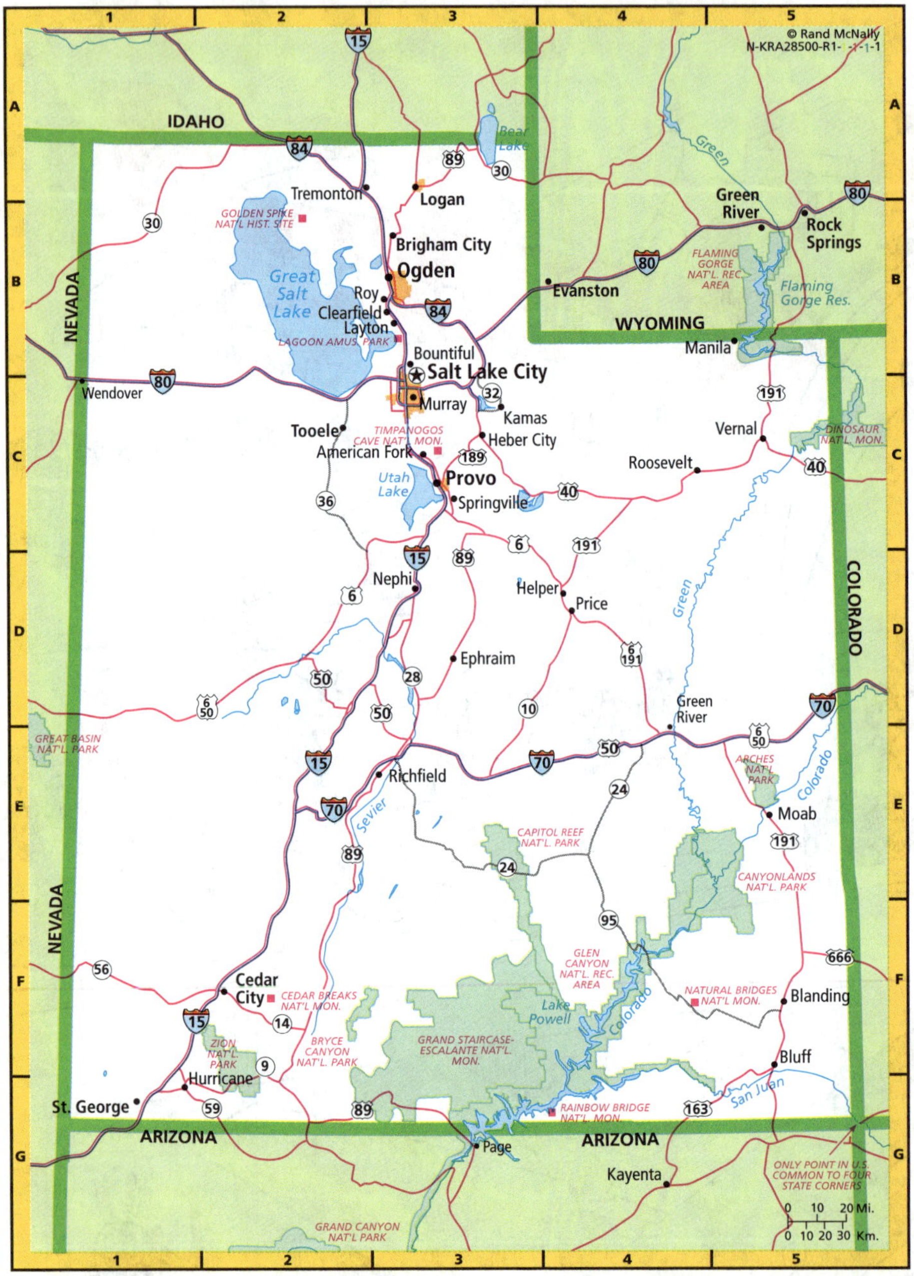

## PARK PLACE

Utah is home to many National Parks and Monuments. Circle the names listed below in the puzzle.

| T | G | R | P | P | H | B | L | S | T | I | Y | T |
|---|---|---|---|---|---|---|---|---|---|---|---|---|
| T | L | I | N | E | S | A | R | C | H | E | S | C |
| A | E | B | A | O | R | E | Z | Q | R | O | M | H |
| Z | N | N | T | P | D | I | N | O | S | A | U | R |
| R | C | O | U | L | E | N | N | B | K | I | R | I |
| O | A | O | R | E | F | G | S | G | N | T | A | S |
| L | N | T | A | O | E | X | D | O | Z | B | D | Q |
| N | Y | F | L | F | G | G | I | L | L | I | B | K |
| G | O | G | B | E | C | W | N | D | A | W | O | E |
| L | N | K | R | A | P | S | H | E | C | V | Y | N |
| A | S | T | I | R | D | O | U | N | H | R | R | D |
| D | D | A | D | T | E | N | D | S | B | O | C | R |
| E | T | E | G | H | V | P | L | P | A | I | H | A |
| N | X | R | E | O | Y | T | S | I | M | I | S | I |
| S | F | R | S | K | B | R | A | K | N | S | O | V |
| C | A | P | I | T | O | L | R | E | E | F | G | S |
| M | G | I | L | K | B | I | I | J | R | I | O | O |
| A | Q | R | L | E | B | S | H | O | A | O | N | G |
| O | J | C | R | A | Y | A | D | C | L | N | A | H |
| C | A | N | Y | O | N | L | A | N | D | S | P | C |
| T | A | H | H | R | N | I | M | L | A | W | M | I |
| R | C | A | L | E | X | S | Y | T | L | P | I | N |
| S | K | A | E | R | B | R | A | D | E | C | T | C |

ARCHES
CANYONLANDS
CAPITOL REEF
CEDAR BREAKS
DINOSAUR
GLEN CANYON
GOLDEN SPIKE
NATURAL BRIDGES
TIMPANOGOS
ZION

Green Mountain State

Capital: Montpelier

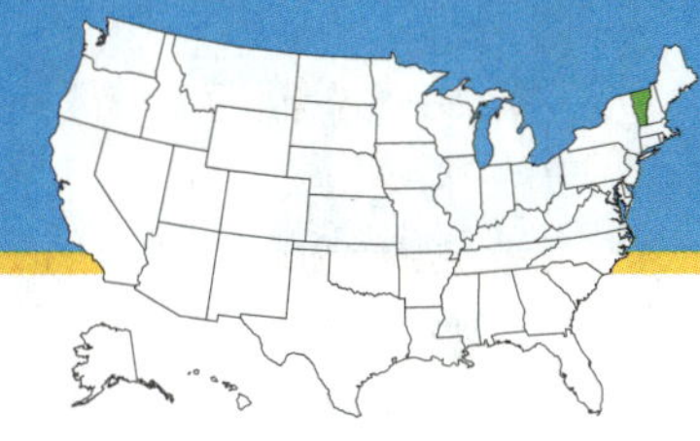

Sugar Maple

Red Clover

Hermit Thrush

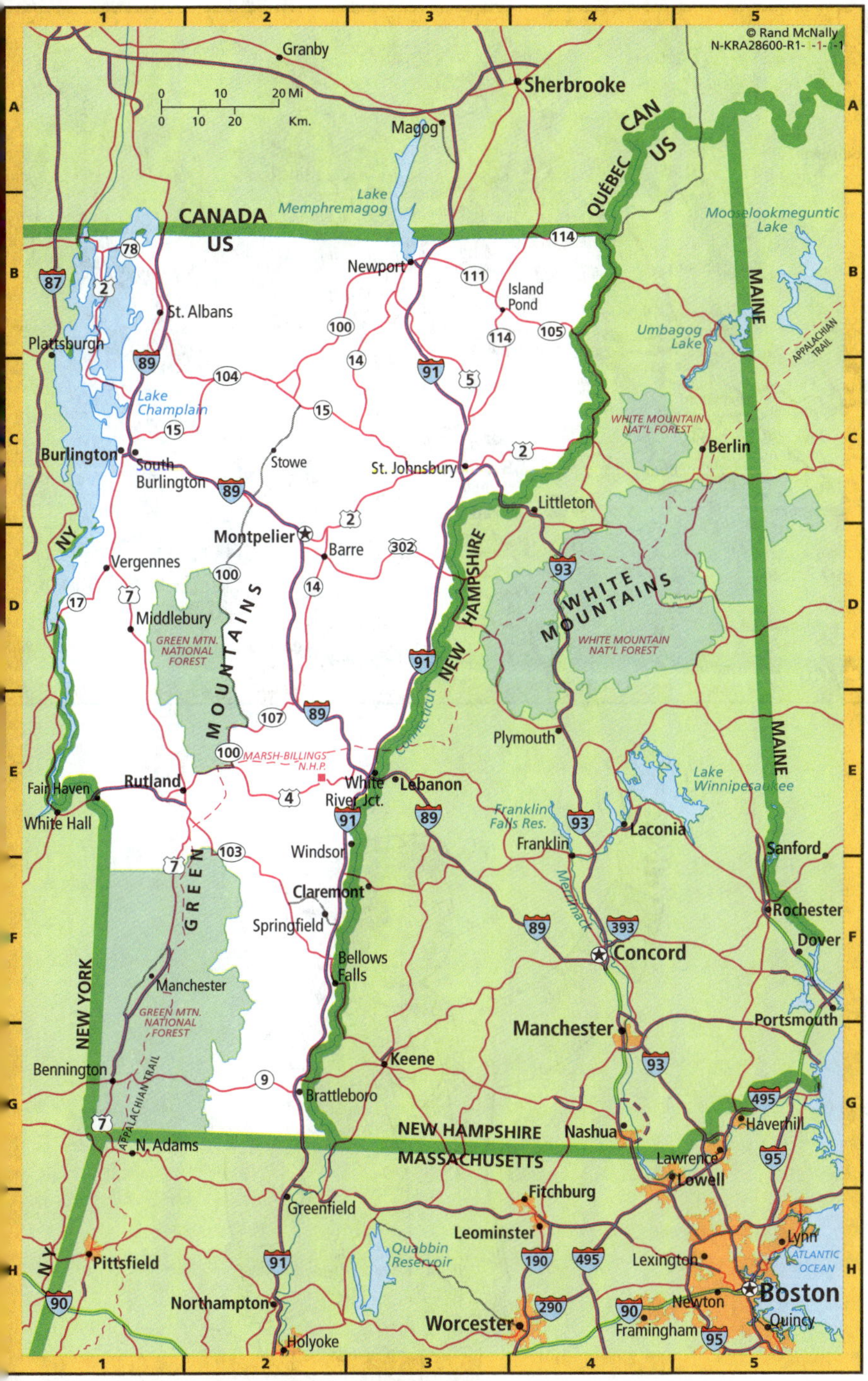

# Unbelievable

All of the facts about Vermont below are true...except for one. To find out which one is not true, solve the equation. The value of X will equal the number next to the false statement.

1. Native Americans taught Europeans how to tap maple trees for syrup.
2. Only Alaska and Wyoming have fewer residents than Vermont.
3. Vermont was once its own country, with its own money!
4. Grandma Moses, a Vermont painter, worked until she was 101 years old.
5. Ice cream from Vermont is popular because cows there have a higher cream content in their milk.

X = The number of the false fact

$X = A - B + C$

$A = B + 4$

$B = C + 2$

$C = 1$

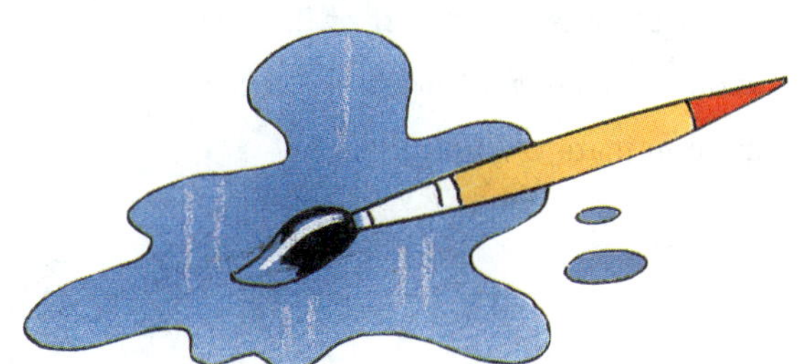

# VirginiA

Old Dominion

Capital:
Richmond

Dogwood

Dogwood Blossom

Cardinal

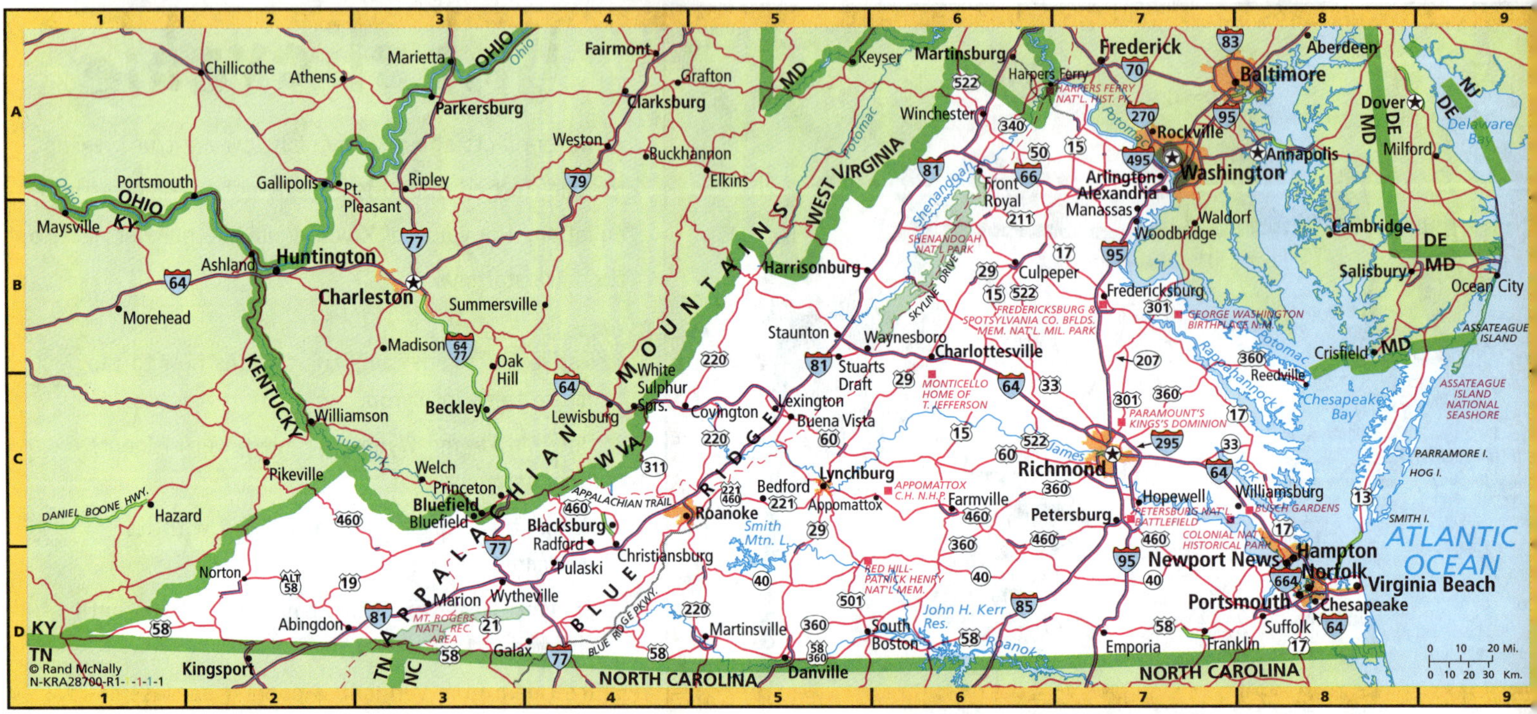

This Virginia city was the center of politics and culture in colonial times. Use the clues to find out the name of this city.

1. It's about 50 miles southeast of Richmond.
2. It's about 35 miles northwest of Norfolk.
3. It's at coordinate C-7.

The city is ____________________________.

# WAshington

Evergreen State

Capital: Olympia

Western Hemlock

Coast Rhododendron

Willow Goldfinch

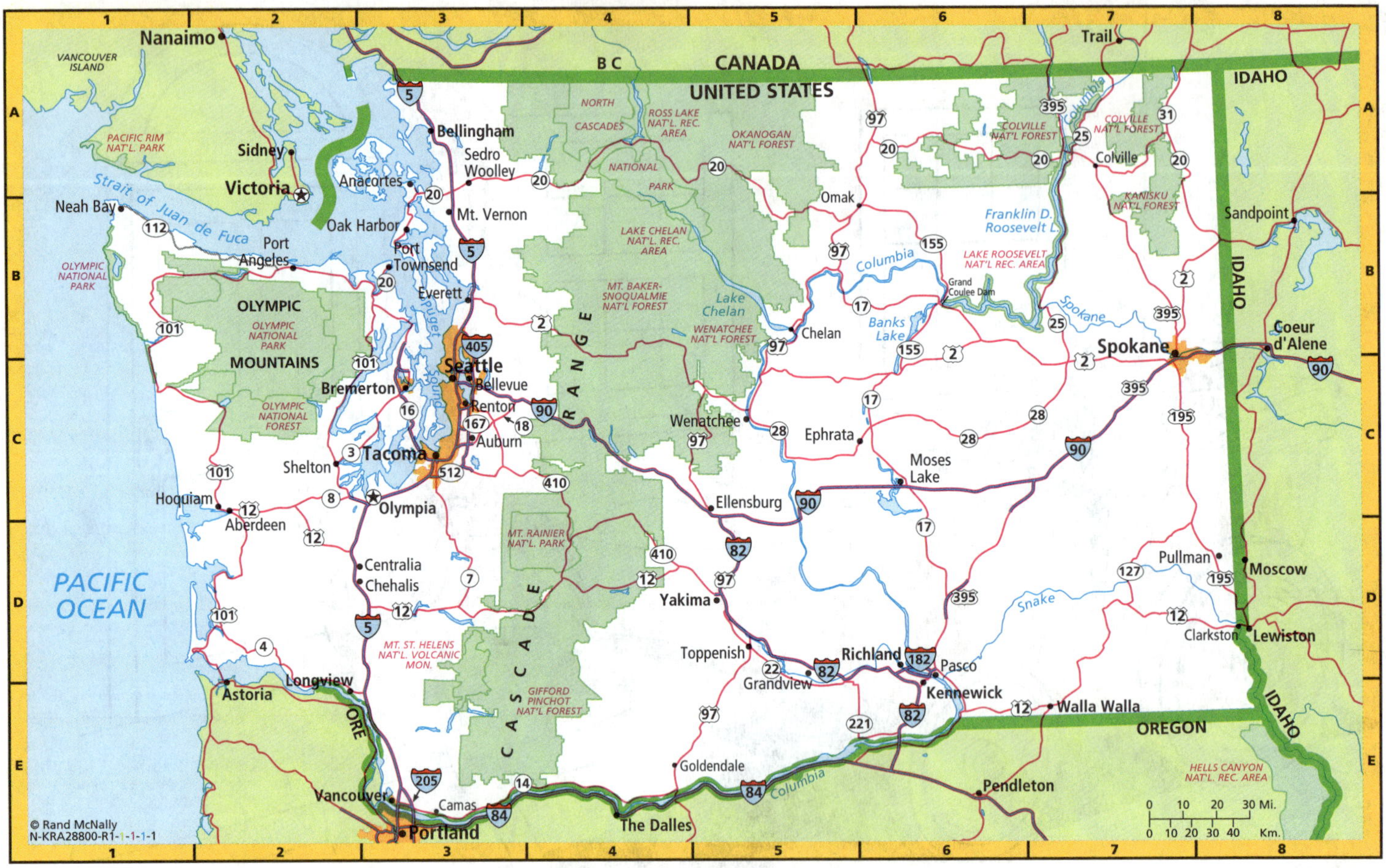

CANADA
UNITED STATES
B C
IDAHO
OREGON
ORE
PACIFIC OCEAN
VANCOUVER ISLAND
Strait of Juan de Fuca
Puget Sound
CASCADE RANGE
OLYMPIC MOUNTAINS
PACIFIC RIM NAT'L. PARK
OLYMPIC NATIONAL PARK
OLYMPIC NATIONAL FOREST
NORTH CASCADES NATIONAL PARK
ROSS LAKE NAT'L. REC. AREA
OKANOGAN NAT'L FOREST
LAKE CHELAN NAT'L. REC. AREA
MT. BAKER-SNOQUALMIE NAT'L FOREST
WENATCHEE NAT'L FOREST
MT. RAINIER NAT'L. PARK
MT. ST. HELENS NAT'L VOLCANIC MON.
GIFFORD PINCHOT NAT'L FOREST
COLVILLE NAT'L FOREST
KANISKU NAT'L FOREST
LAKE ROOSEVELT NAT'L REC. AREA
HELLS CANYON NAT'L. REC. AREA
Franklin D. Roosevelt L.
Grand Coulee Dam
Lake Chelan
Banks Lake
Columbia
Spokane
Snake
Nanaimo
Sidney
Victoria
Neah Bay
Port Angeles
Anacortes
Oak Harbor
Port Townsend
Bellingham
Sedro Woolley
Mt. Vernon
Everett
Seattle
Bellevue
Renton
Auburn
Bremerton
Tacoma
Shelton
Olympia
Hoquiam
Aberdeen
Centralia
Chehalis
Astoria
Longview
Vancouver
Portland
Camas
The Dalles
Goldendale
Yakima
Toppenish
Grandview
Richland
Pasco
Kennewick
Walla Walla
Pendleton
Ellensburg
Wenatchee
Chelan
Ephrata
Moses Lake
Omak
Colville
Trail
Spokane
Coeur d'Alene
Sandpoint
Pullman
Moscow
Clarkston
Lewiston
0 10 20 30 Mi.
0 10 20 30 40 Km.
© Rand McNally
N-KRA28800-R1-1-1-1-1

# Picture Quiz

Write the last letters of the objects below in the boxes. When you're finished, the letters will spell out the name of an event that was started in 1909 by Sonora Louise Smart Dodd in Spokane, Washington.

____ ____ ____ ____ ____ ____ ____ ,

____ ____ ____

# West Virginia

Mountain State

Capital: Charleston

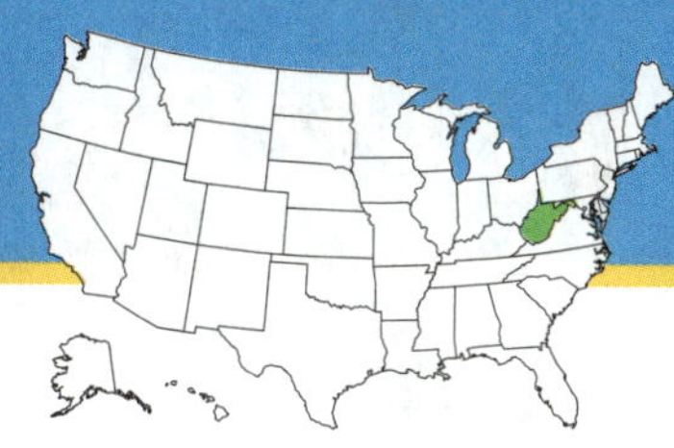

Sugar Maple

Rhododendron

Cardinal

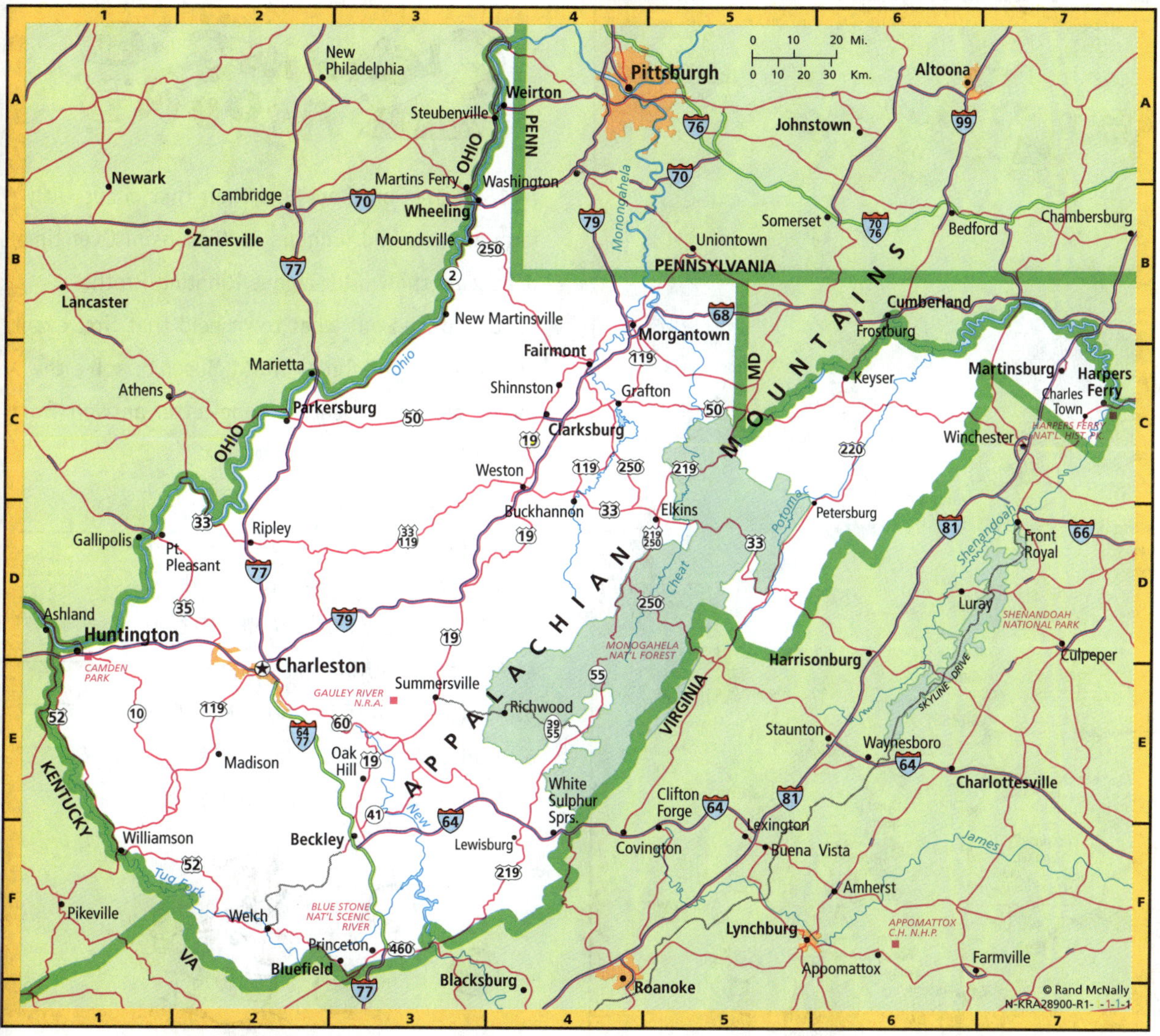

Cross out the words that answer the clues. An interesting fact about West Virginia will be left when you're finished.

LUES

. The town directly across the river from Steubenville
. The river that makes up most of the west border
. The town that is "NOT SEW" scrambled
. The "dishonest" river
. The town that is the farthest east
. The river that George Washington threw a dollar over
. The river that makes up part of the southwestern border
. The state that borders West Virginia to the southwest
. The state capital

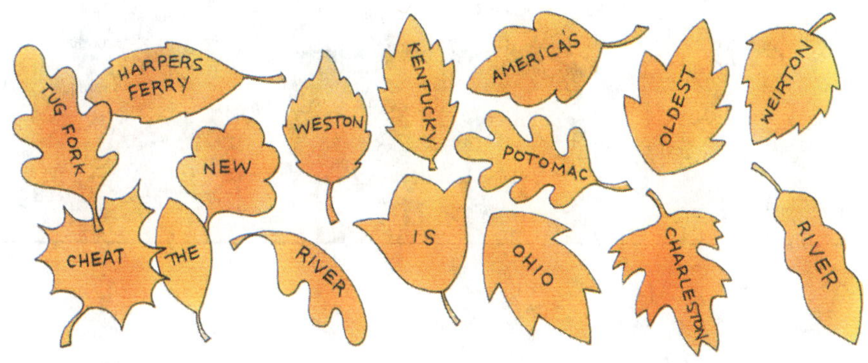

# Wisconsin

Badger State

Capital: Madison

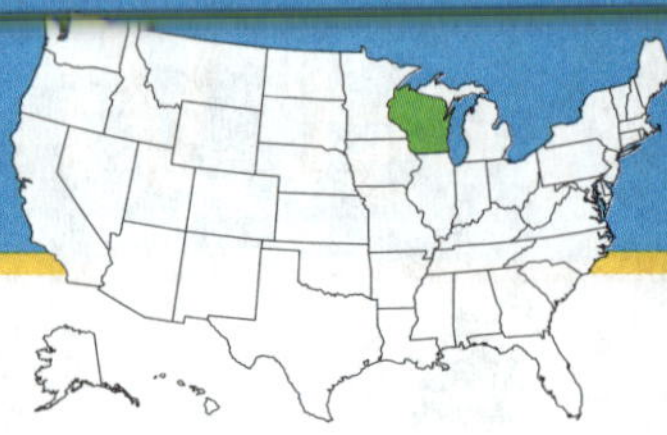

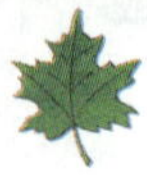

Sugar Maple

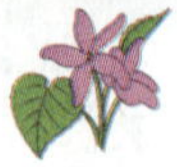

Wood Violet

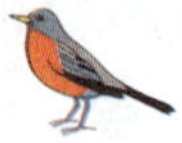

Robin

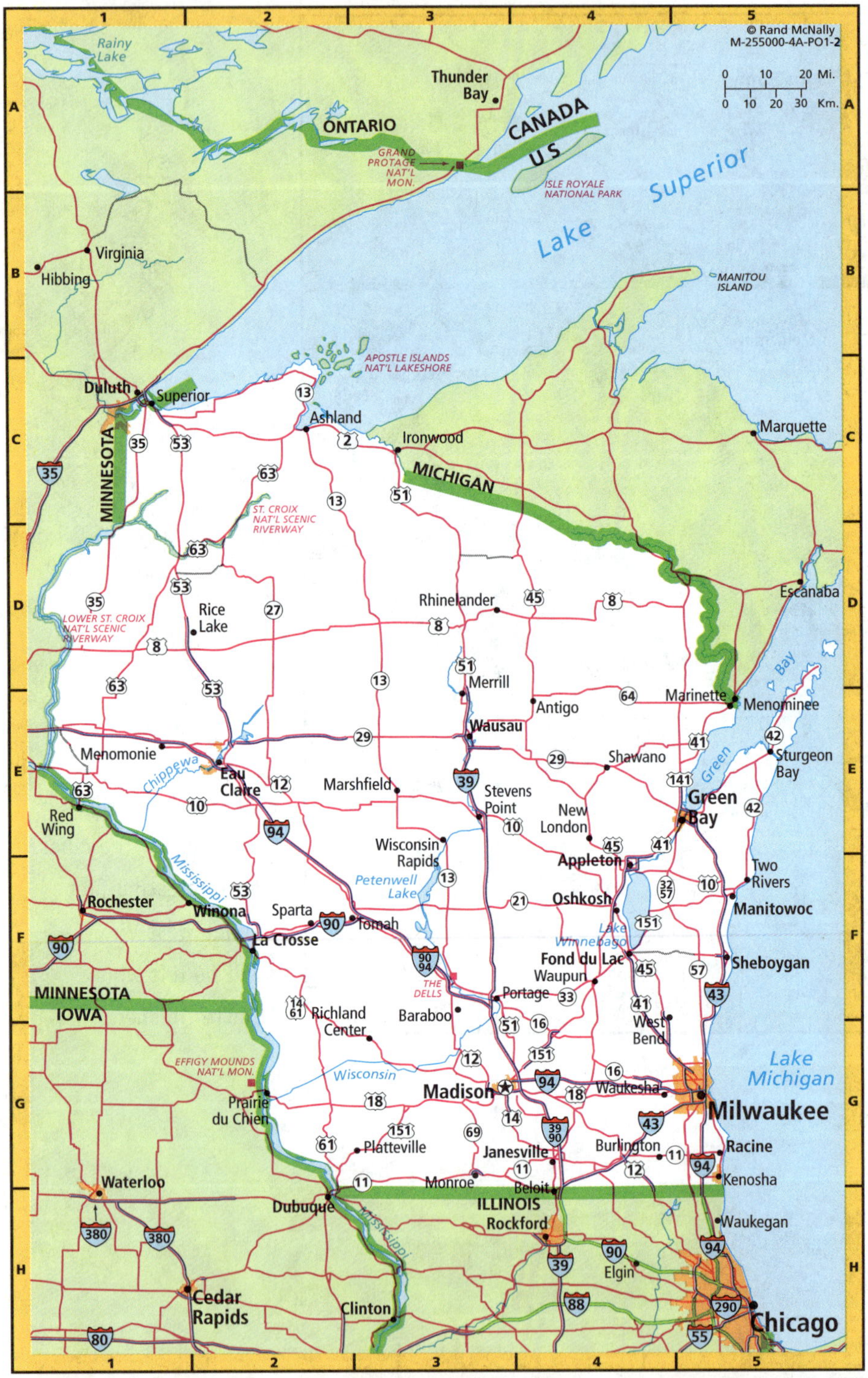


## Clowning Around

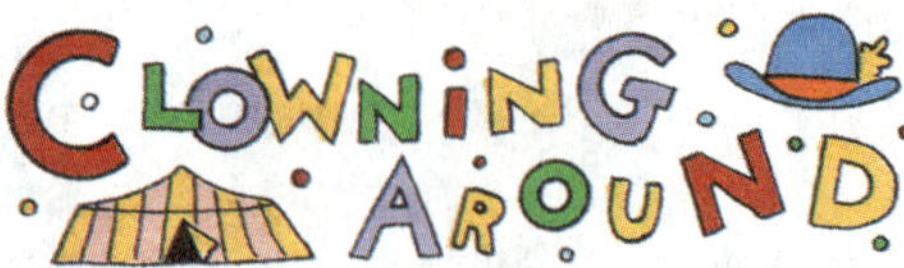

In 1884, five brothers held their first circus with farm animals and jugglers in Wisconsin. Over time, it became the world famous Ringling Brothers Circus. To find out what town held that first event, and now has the Circus World Museum, solve the puzzle below and read the one-letter answers from top to bottom.

1. A letter in BEAR but not in TRAPEZE _____
2. A letter in LAKE and MICHIGAN _____
3. A letter in SPARTA and MERRILL _____
4. A letter in SUGAR and MAPLE _____
5. A letter in BRIE but not AMERICAN _____
6. A letter in HOLSTEIN and COW _____
7. A letter in TRACTOR but not CART _____

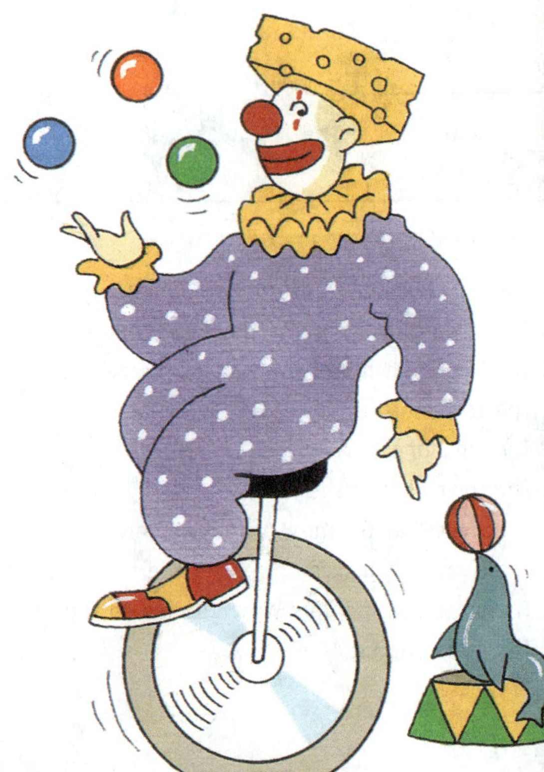

# WYoming

Equality State

Capital: Cheyenne

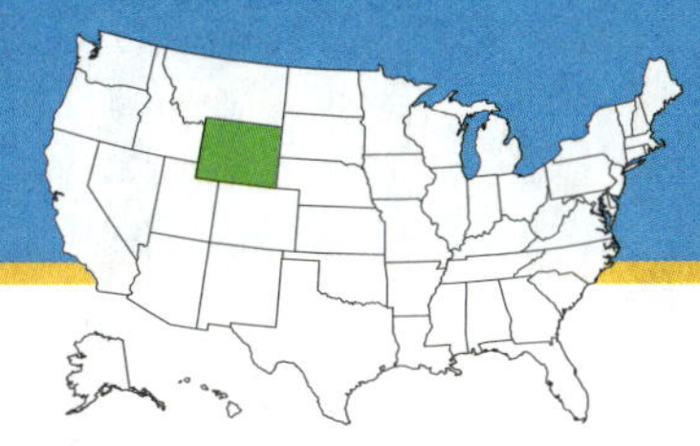

Cottonwood

Indian Paintbrush

Western Meadowlark

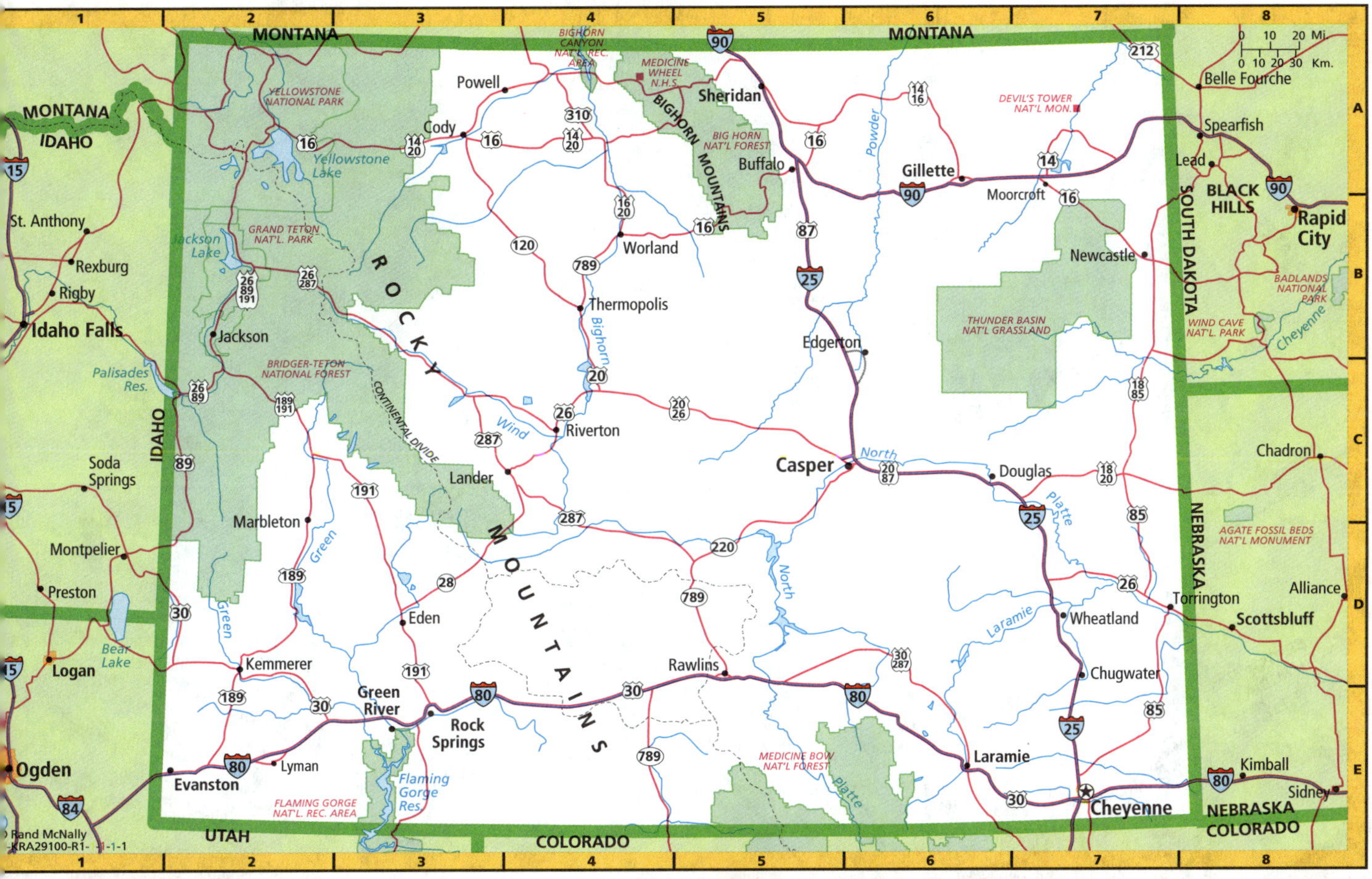

SEE YOU AT THE TOP!

Climb to the top! Start at the bottom left and see if you can make it to the top of Devil's Tower (A–7).

# Canada

Capital:
Ottawa

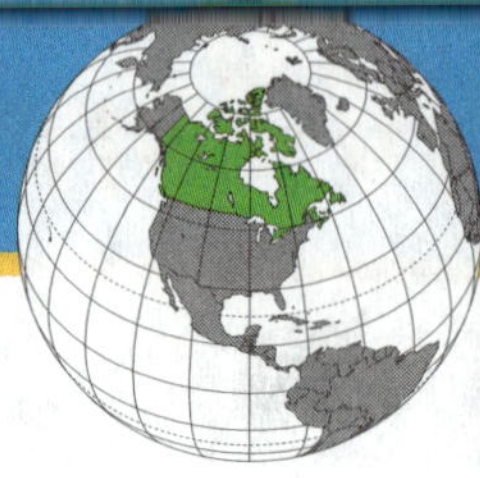

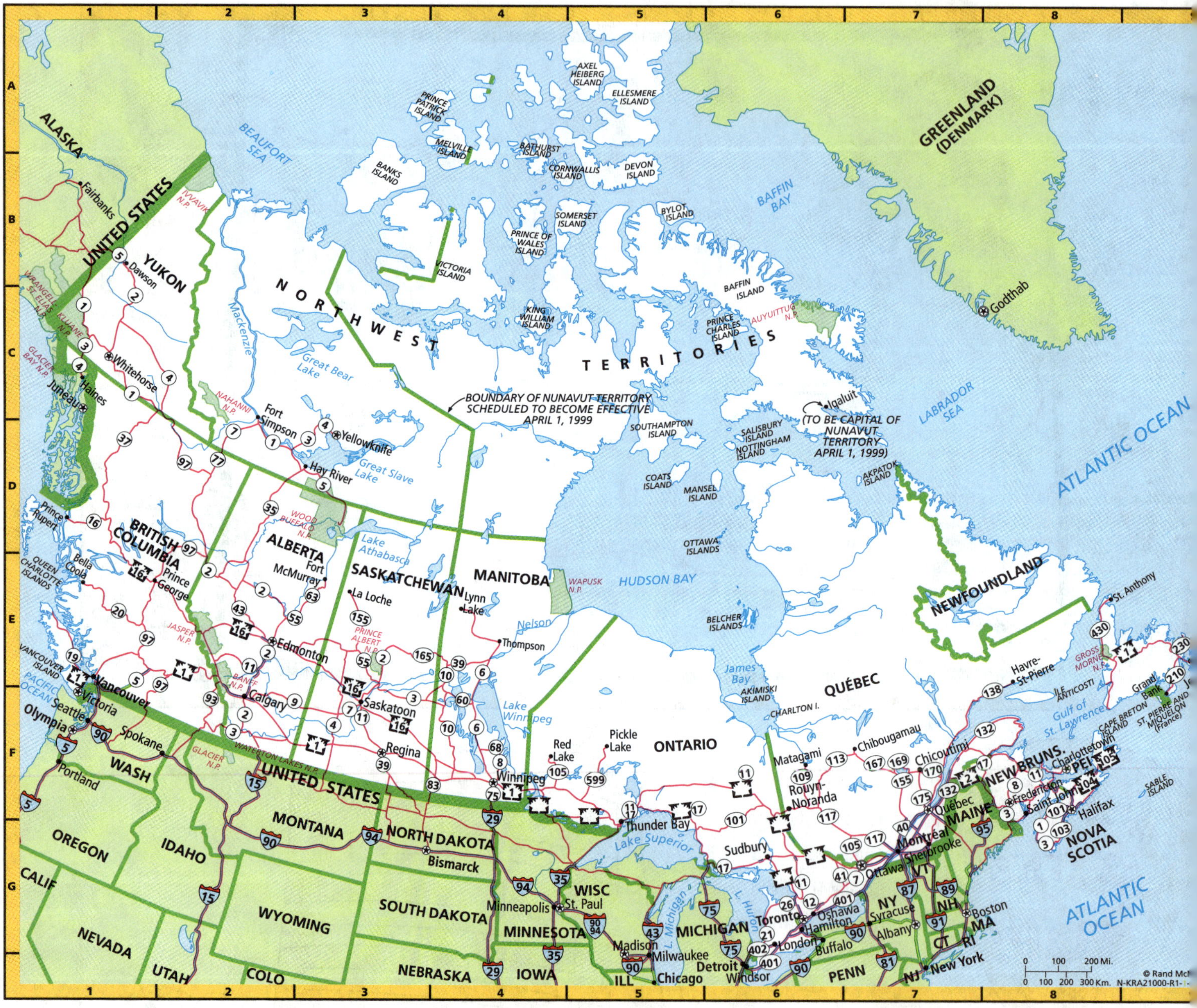

1 2 3 4 5 6 7 8

A B C D E F G

ALASKA
Fairbanks
UNITED STATES
YUKON
Dawson
Whitehorse
Haines
Juneau
WRANGELL-ST. ELIAS N.P.
KLUANE N.P.
GLACIER BAY N.P.
IVVAVIK N.P.
BEAUFORT SEA
Mackenzie
NORTHWEST TERRITORIES
Great Bear Lake
NAHANNI N.P.
Fort Simpson
Yellowknife
Great Slave Lake
Hay River
BOUNDARY OF NUNAVUT TERRITORY SCHEDULED TO BECOME EFFECTIVE APRIL 1, 1999
PRINCE PATRICK ISLAND
MELVILLE ISLAND
BANKS ISLAND
VICTORIA ISLAND
AXEL HEIBERG ISLAND
ELLESMERE ISLAND
BATHURST ISLAND
CORNWALLIS ISLAND
DEVON ISLAND
SOMERSET ISLAND
PRINCE OF WALES ISLAND
KING WILLIAM ISLAND
BYLOT ISLAND
BAFFIN BAY
BAFFIN ISLAND
PRINCE CHARLES ISLAND
AUYUITTUQ N.P.
GREENLAND (DENMARK)
Godthab
Iqaluit
(TO BE CAPITAL OF NUNAVUT TERRITORY APRIL 1, 1999)
SOUTHAMPTON ISLAND
SALISBURY ISLAND
NOTTINGHAM ISLAND
COATS ISLAND
MANSEL ISLAND
AKPATOK ISLAND
LABRADOR SEA
ATLANTIC OCEAN
Prince Rupert
QUEEN CHARLOTTE ISLANDS
BRITISH COLUMBIA
Bella Coola
Prince George
VANCOUVER ISLAND
PACIFIC OCEAN
Vancouver
Victoria
Seattle
Olympia
Spokane
Portland
ALBERTA
WOOD BUFFALO N.P.
Fort McMurray
JASPER N.P.
Edmonton
BANFF N.P.
Calgary
GLACIER N.P.
WATERTON LAKES N.P.
SASKATCHEWAN
Lake Athabasca
La Loche
PRINCE ALBERT N.P.
Saskatoon
Regina
MANITOBA
Lynn Lake
Thompson
Nelson
Lake Winnipeg
Winnipeg
WAPUSK N.P.
HUDSON BAY
OTTAWA ISLANDS
BELCHER ISLANDS
James Bay
AKIMISKI ISLAND
CHARLTON I.
ONTARIO
Red Lake
Pickle Lake
Thunder Bay
Lake Superior
Sudbury
L. Michigan
L. Huron
Toronto
Oshawa
Hamilton
London
Windsor
Detroit
Ottawa
QUÉBEC
Matagami
Rouyn-Noranda
Chibougamau
Chicoutimi
Québec
Montréal
Sherbrooke
NEWFOUNDLAND
St. Anthony
GROS MORNE N.P.
Havre-St-Pierre
ILE ANTICOSTI
Gulf of St. Lawrence
Grand Bank
ST. PIERRE AND MIQUELON (France)
CAPE BRETON ISLAND
NEW BRUNS.
Fredericton
Saint John
P.E.I.
Charlottetown
Halifax
NOVA SCOTIA
SABLE ISLAND
WASH
OREGON
CALIF
NEVADA
IDAHO
UTAH
MONTANA
WYOMING
COLO
NORTH DAKOTA
Bismarck
SOUTH DAKOTA
NEBRASKA
MINNESOTA
Minneapolis
St. Paul
IOWA
WISC
Madison
Milwaukee
Chicago
ILL
MICHIGAN
NY
Syracuse
Albany
Buffalo
PENN
New York
NJ
VT
NH
MA
Boston
CT
RI
MAINE
0 100 200 Mi.
0 100 200 300 Km.
© Rand McNally N-KRA21000-R1-

# TAKE A GANDER!

Hey! That Canada goose shouldn't be flying upside down!
How many other mistakes can you find in this Canadian scene?

Capital:
Mexico City

UNITED STATES
US
San Diego
Tijuana
Mexicali
Ensenada
San Felípe
BAJA CALIF
Bahia Sebastian Vizcaino
ISLA CEDROS
SONORA
Hermosillo
Gulf of California
Ciudad Juárez
Rio Grande
Chihuahua
CHIHUAHUA
Ciudad Obregón
Los Mochis
SINALOA
BAJA CALIF SUR
San Carlos
La Paz
San José del Cabo
PACIFIC OCEAN
Culiacán
DURANGO
Durango
Mazatlán
COAHUILA
Monclova
Torreón
Monterrey
Saltillo
NUEVO LEON
Nuevo Laredo
Reynosa
Matamoros
TAMAULIPAS
Ciudad Victoria
ZACATECAS
Zacatecas
SAN LUIS POTOSI
San Luis Potosi
Tampico
NAYARIT
Tepic
ISLAS TRES MARIAS
AGS
Aguascalientes
León
GTO
QRO
Querétaro
HGO
Pachuca
Guadalajara
JALISCO
COLIMA
MICHOACÁN
Morelia
Uruapan del Progreso
MÉX
Mexico City
TLAX
MOR
Puebla
PUEBLA
Poza Rica
VERACRUZ
Xalapa
Veracruz
Orizaba
GUERRERO
Acapulco
OAXACA
Oaxaca
Balsas
Gulf of Tehuantepec
BAY OF CAMPECHE
GULF OF MEXIC
TABASCO
Villahermosa
CAMPECHE
Campeche
Mèrida
CHIAPAS
Tuxtla Gutièrrez
Presa de la Angostura
GUATEMA
Guatemala
Dallas
Houston
New Orleans
BIG BEND NAT'L PARK
Int'l. Amistad Res.
PARQUE NAC. DEL GRAN DESIERTO DEL PINACATE
PARQUE NAC. CUMBRES DE MAJALACA
PARQUE NACIONAL BARRANCA DEL COBRE
PARQUE INTERNACIONAL DEL RÍO BRAVO LOS NOVILLOS
PARQUE NACIONAL LOS NOVILLOS
PARQUE NACIONAL MISOL-HA
PARQUE NACION LAGUNAS DE MONTEBELLO
0 40 80 120 Mi.
0 80 160 Km.
© Rand McNally
N-KRA32000-R1-1-1-1-1

1. This body of water is to the east of Quintana Roo.
2. This city is directly south of San Diego, California.
3. This state on the south of the Bay of Campeche has the same name as a spicy sauce.
4. This food is a flat bread made from corn.
5. This river, or *rio*, forms much of the border between Mexico and the U.S.
6. This cliff-diving location is the southernmost point on 95D.
7. This city's name is a combination of Mexico and California.
8. This state in northern Mexico shares its name with a breed of dogs.
9. This body of water lies west of the Baja Peninsula.
10. This country lies east of the Chiapas.
11. As you take 45 north, the last city you go through befo leaving Mexico is _______.
12. This city is directly across the border to the north of #1
13. This country is south of Quintana Roo.
14. This "little beautiful" city is a major one in Sonora.

# SOUTH of the BORDER

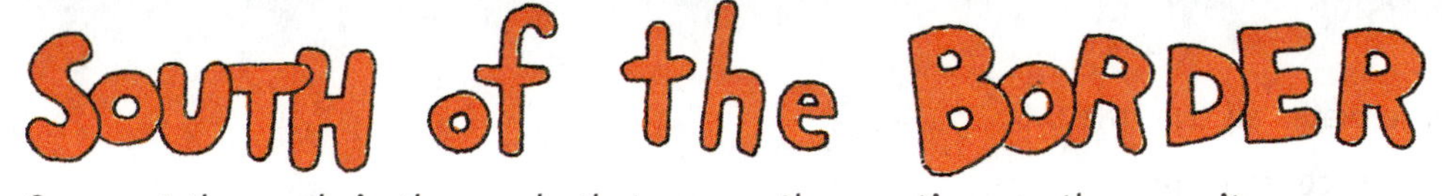

Cross out the words in the puzzle that answer the questions on the opposite page.

An interesting fact about Mexico will be left when you're finished. Read it from top to bottom.

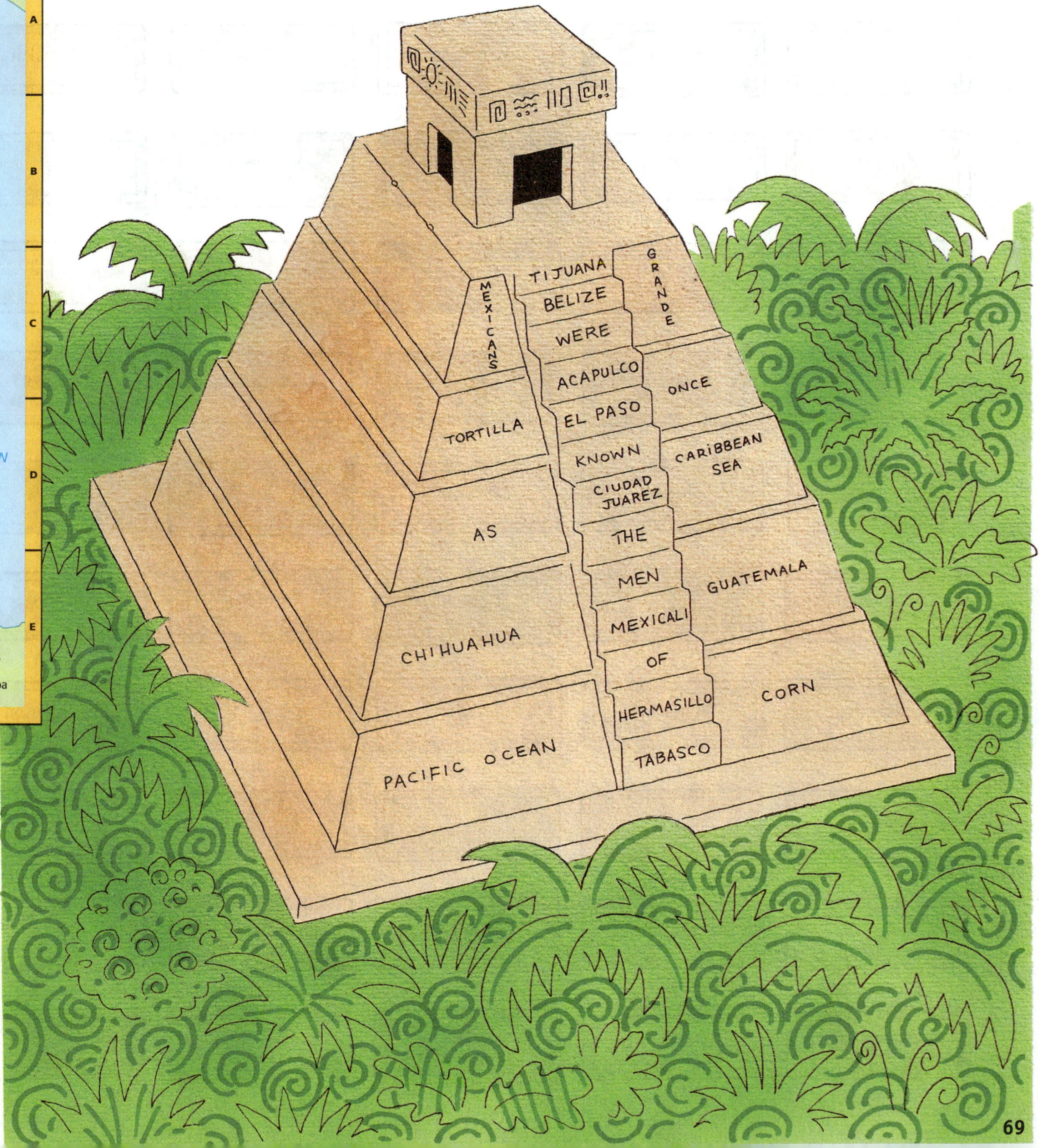

MEXICANS
TIJUANA
GRANDE
BELIZE
WERE
ACAPULCO
ONCE
TORTILLA
EL PASO
KNOWN
CARIBBEAN SEA
CIUDAD JUAREZ
AS
THE
MEN
GUATEMALA
CHIHUAHUA
MEXICALI
OF
CORN
HERMASILLO
PACIFIC OCEAN
TABASCO


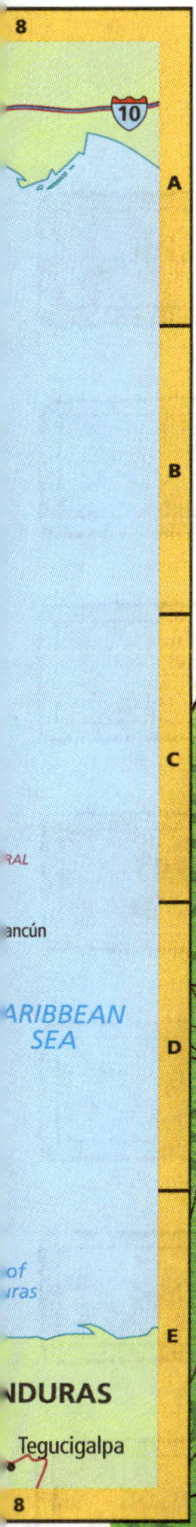

10
ARIBBEAN SEA
NDURAS
Tegucigalpa

# License Plate Game

Keep an eye out for license plates all over the U.S.
Cross off the state when you see its plate.

# Answers

## Using an Atlas

Pages 4–5
Everglades; Florida; Denver; Colorado; Newport Beach; California; Tijuana
The adventure begins with a turn of the page!

## United States

Page 7
1. AL; 2. AK; 3. AZ; 4. AR; 5. CA; 6. CO; 7. CT; 8. DE; 9. FL; 10. GA; 11. HI; 12. ID; 13. IL; 14. IN; 15. IA; 16. KS; 17. KY; 18. LA; 19. ME; 20. MD; 21. MA; 22. MI; 23. MN; 24. MS; 25. MO; 26. MT; 27. NE; 28. NV; 29. NH; 30. NJ; 31. NM; 32. NY; 33. NC; 34. ND; 35. OH; 36. OK; 37. OR; 38. PA; 39. RI; 40. SC; 41. SD; 42. TN; 43. TX; 44. UT; 45. VT; 46. VA; 47. WA; 48. WV; 49. WI; 50. WY

## Alabama

Page 8
Huntsville, Alabama

## Alaska

Page 9

ALASKA

## Arizona

Page 10
How deep?
40 ÷ 10 = 4 Empire State Buildings (up to 5,500 feet deep)
How long?
191 + 80 – 64 + 10 = 217 miles long (Illinois is 218 miles wide)

## Arkansas

Page 11
Stuttgart, Pine Bluff, Camden, Magnolia, El Dorado, Crosset, Monticello

## California

Page 13
1. Redwood; 2. Sequoia; 3. Joshua Tree; 4. Yosemite; 5. Kings Canyon; 6. Death Valley
State Motto: "Eureka!"

## Colorado

Page 14
C–3 Aspen; B–5 Boulder; B–3 Rifle; A–3 Steamboat Springs; B–6 Brush; A–2 Dinosaur National Monument; A–6 Crow River; C–5 Castle Rock

## Connecticut

Page 15

## Delaware

Page 16

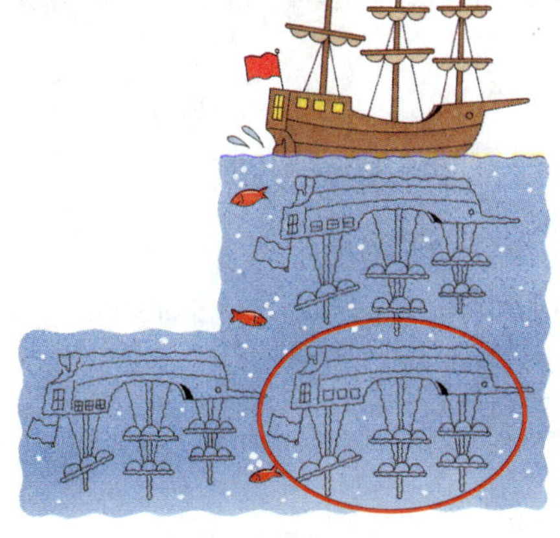

## Florida

Page 17
OCEAN and CANOE; PALM and LAMP; PEARS and SPEAR; MELON and LEMON; TEN and NET; SHOE and HOSE; BEARD and BREAD

## Georgia

Page 18

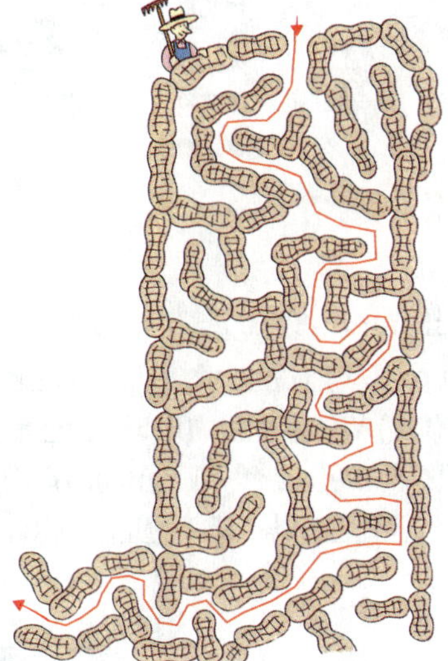

## Hawaii

Page 19
Kilauea is an active volcano in Hawaii Volcanoes National Park.

# Answers

## Idaho

Page 20

IDAHO

## Illinois

Page 21

1. Paris; 2. Beardstown;
3. Sandwich; 4. Rock Falls;
5. Normal; 6. Champaign

## Indiana

Page 22

1st—#8 Yellow; 2nd—#2 Orange; 3rd—#10 Red

## Iowa

Page 24

More popcorn is produced in Sioux City, Iowa, than in any other place in the world.

## Kansas

Page 25

## Kentucky

Page 26

(C-3) Owensboro; (C-5) Louisville; (C-5) Shelbyville; (C-6) Lawrenceburg; (C-6) Frankfort; (C-6) Harrodsburg; (C-7) Richmond; (C-7) Winchester; (D-5) Campbellsville; (D-6) Danville; (D-7) London; (D-8) Harlan; (D-8) Pikeville; (E-2) Murray; (E-4) Russellville; (E-6) Monticello; (E-7) Williamsburg; (E-7) Middlesboro

## Louisiana

Page 27

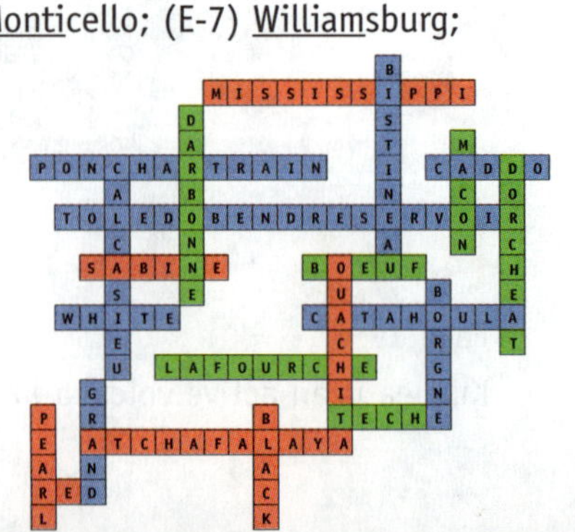


## Maine

Page 28

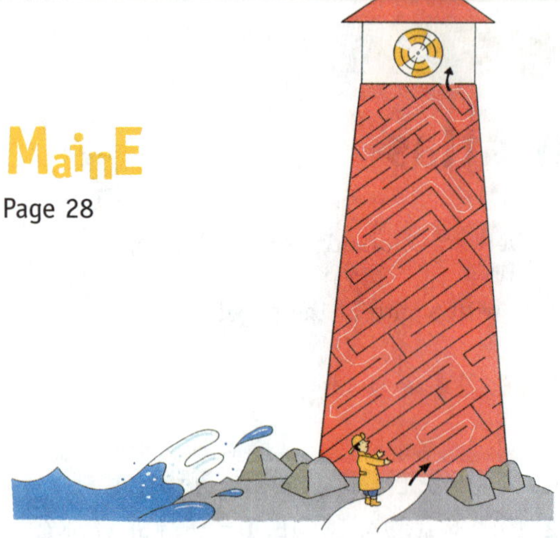

## Maryland

Page 29

He was a prisoner on a British ship.

## Massachusetts

Page 31

## Michigan

Page 32

## Minnesota

Page 33

Across: 3. Mille; 4. Vermillion; 6. Leech

Down: 1. Upper Red; 2. Winnibigoshish; 5. Itasca; 6. Lower Red

## Mississippi

Page 34

paddlewheel, post, pier, pirate, patch (eye), parrot, pegleg, pipe, picnic, plate, paw, person, pants, pig, pony, pineapple, pillow, palm tree, pail, path, park bench, pepper, park, puddle, periscope, poodle, paddle, plane, pencil, pelican, parking meter

## Missouri

Page 35

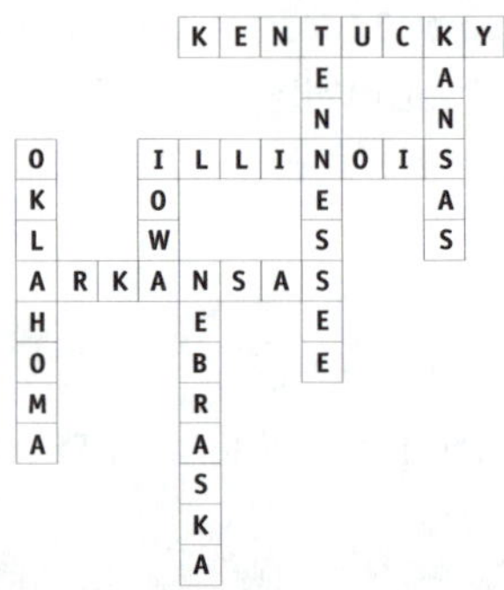

# Answers

## MonTana

age 36

## NEbraska

age 37

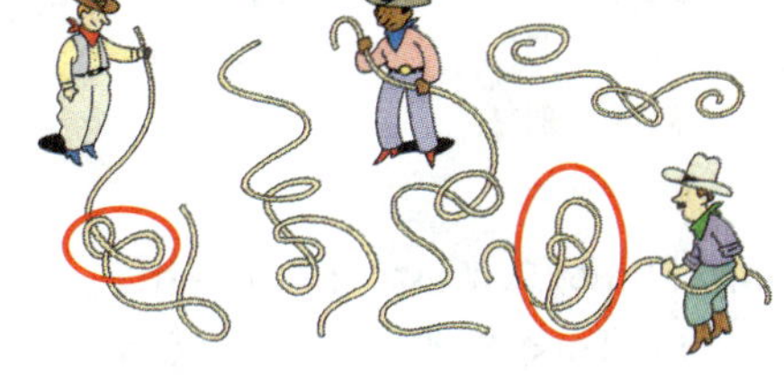

## NeVada

age 38

as Vegas

## New Hampshire

age 39

hip, ramp, shrimp, wasp, man, pines, hen, map, harp, pear, ie, peas, sheep, saw

## New Jersey

age 40

## New Mexico

age 41

NEW JERSEY

NEW MEXICO

## New York

age 43

nail box, periscope, sail boat on rock, snow boarder, candy cane, chimney on tent, fishing in fire, fire hydrant, dolphin in stream, shoe in tree

## North Carolina

age 44

rog, flashlight, fish, fin (on fish), flamingo, feather, fire or lame, fruit, flower, farmer, fan, flippers, football, fork, oot/feet, face, forehead, fingers, fringe (on towel or blanket), four (on t-shirt), fence, funnel

## North Dakota

Page 45

1. Bowman; 2. Rugby; 3. Grand Forks; 4. Devils Lake; 5. Valley City; 6. Carrington

## OHio

Page 47

Findlay, Newark, Ashland, Canton, Whitehall, Springfield, Logan, Athens, Portsmouth, Oxford, Fairborn, Middletown

## OKlahoma

Page 48

dine—Enid (A-5); bilead—Idabel (D-8); lowtan—Lawton (C-5); wassail—Sallisaw (B-8); leekomug—Okmulgee (B-7); moungy—Guymon (A-2); usalt—Tulsa (B-7); amimi—Miami (A-8); sheenwa—Shawnee (C-6); talliwerts—Stillwater (B-6)

## ORegon

Page 49

## PennsylVAnia

Page 50

## Rhode Island

Page 51

1. red light; 2. redwood; 3. red, white, and blue; 4. see red; 5. Little Red Riding Hood; 6. red carpet; 7. redhead

## South Carolina

Page 52

# Answers

## South Dakota

Page 53

The correct order is P, E, O, P, L, E, which spells out PEOPLE

## Tennessee

Page 54

## Texas

Page 57

## Utah

Page 58

| T | G | R | P | P | H | B | L | S | T | I | Y | T |
|---|---|---|---|---|---|---|---|---|---|---|---|---|
| T | L | I | N | E | S | A | R | C | H | E | S | C |
| A | E | B | A | O | R | E | Z | Q | R | O | M | H |
| Z | N | N | T | P | D | I | N | O | S | A | U | R |
| R | C | O | U | L | E | N | N | B | K | I | R | I |
| O | A | O | R | E | F | G | S | G | N | T | A | S |
| L | N | T | A | O | E | X | D | O | Z | B | D | Q |
| N | Y | F | L | F | G | G | I | L | L | I | B | K |
| G | O | G | B | E | C | W | N | D | A | W | O | E |
| L | N | K | R | A | P | S | H | E | C | V | Y | N |
| A | S | T | I | R | D | O | U | N | H | R | R | D |
| D | D | A | D | T | E | N | D | S | B | O | C | R |
| E | T | E | G | H | V | P | L | P | A | I | H | A |
| N | X | R | E | O | Y | T | S | I | M | I | S | I |
| S | F | R | S | K | B | R | A | K | N | S | O | V |
| C | A | P | I | T | O | L | R | E | E | F | G | S |
| M | G | I | L | K | B | I | I | J | R | I | O | O |
| A | Q | R | L | E | B | S | H | O | A | O | N | G |
| O | J | C | R | A | Y | A | D | C | L | N | A | H |
| C | A | N | Y | O | N | L | A | N | D | S | P | C |
| T | A | H | H | R | N | I | M | L | A | W | M | I |
| R | C | A | L | E | X | S | Y | T | L | P | I | N |
| S | K | A | E | R | B | R | A | D | E | C | T | C |

UTAH

## Vermont

Page 59

A = 7; B = 3; C = 1; X = 5

Fact number 5 is false.

## Virginia

Page 60

Williamsburg

## Washington

Page 62

Sonora Louise Smart Dodd started Father's Day.

## West Virginia

Page 63

1. Weirton; 2. Ohio; 3. Weston; 4. Cheat; 5. Harper's Ferry; 6. Potomac; 7. Tug Fork; 8. Kentucky; 9. Charleston

Fact: The New River is America's oldest river.

## Wisconsin

Page 64

1. B; 2. A; 3. R; 4. A; 5. B; 6. O; 7. O

## Wyoming

## Canada

Page 67

## Mexico

Page 69

"Mexicans were once know as men of corn."

## labama
p on page 8
oulation estimate: 4,335,400
a: 50,750 sq. mi.



## laska
p on page 9
oulation estimate: 611,500
a: 570,374 sq. mi.



## Arizona
Map on page 10
Population estimate: 4,664,600
Area: 113,642 sq. mi.



## Arkansas
Map on page 11
Population estimate: 2,531,000
Area: 52,075 sq. mi.



## California
Map on page 12
Population estimate: 33,198,100
Area: 155,973 sq. mi.



## Colorado
Map on page 14
Population estimate: 3,930,700
Area: 103,730 sq. mi.



## Connecticut
Map on page 15
Population estimate: 3,271,100
Area: 4,845 sq. mi.



## Delaware
Map on page 16
Population estimate: 736,900
Area: 1,955 sq. mi.



## District of Columbia
Map on page 7
Population estimate: 523,800
Area: 61 sq. mi.

## Florida
Map on page 17
Population estimate: 15,012,200
Area: 53,997 sq. mi.



pulation estimates are for the year 2000.

# Index



## Georgia

Map on page 18
Population estimate: 7,562,200
Area: 57,919 sq. mi.



## Hawaii

Map on page 19
Population estimate: 7,562,200
Area: 57,919 sq. mi.



## Idaho

Map on page 20
Population estimate: 1,221,500
Area: 82,751 sq. mi.



## Illinois

Map on page 21
Population estimate: 11,981,700
Area: 55,593 sq. mi.



## Indiana

Map on page 22
Population estimate: 5,882,500
Area: 35,870 sq. mi.



## Iowa

Map on page 24
Population estimate: 2,854,700
Area: 55,875 sq. mi.



## Kansas

Map on page 25
Population estimate: 2,603,200
Area: 81,823 sq. mi.





*Population estimates are for the year 20*

*pulation estimates are for the year 2000.*

# Index



## Montana

Map on page 36
Population estimate: 5,421,400
Area: 68,898 sq. mi.



## Nebraska

Map on page 37
Population estimate: 1,661,400
Area: 76,878 sq. mi.



## Nevada

Map on page 38
Population estimate: 1,828,700
Area: 109,806 sq. mi.



## New Hampshire

Map on page 39
Population estimate: 1,179,100
Area: 8,969 sq. mi.



## New Jersey

Map on page 40
Population estimate: 8,078,300
Area: 7,419 sq. mi.



## New Mexico

Map on page 41
Population estimate: 1,738,700
Area: 121,365 sq. mi.



## New York

Map on page 42
Population estimate: 18,197,800
Area: 47,224 sq. mi.



## North Carolina

Map on page 44
Population estimate: 7,483,100
Area: 48,718 sq. mi.



## North Dakota

(Map on page 45)
Population estimate: 640,000
Area: 68,994 sq. mi.



## Ohio

Map on page 46
Population estimate: 11,197,90
Area: 40,953 sq. mi.





*Population estimates are for the year 20*

## klahoma

on page 48
lation estimate: 3,328,100
: 68,679 sq. mi.



## Oregon

Map on page 49
Population estimate: 3,266,800
Area: 96,003 sq. mi.



## Pennsylvania

Map on page 50
Population estimate: 12,044,200
Area: 44,820 sq. mi.



## Rhode Island

Map on page 51
Population estimate: 987,000
Area: 1,045 sq. mi.



## South Carolina

Map on page 52
Population estimate: 3,781,800
Area: 30,111 sq. mi.



## South Dakota

Map on page 53
Population estimate: 738,500
Area: 75,898 sq. mi.



## Tennessee

Map on page 54
Population estimate: 5,398,200
Area: 41,220 sq. mi.



## Texas

Map on page 56
Population estimate: 19,613,400
Area: 261,914 sq. mi.



ulation estimates are for the year 2000.

# Index



## Utah

Map on page 58
Population estimate: 2,071,500
Area: 82,168 sq. mi.



## Vermont

Map on page 59
Population estimate: 590,400
Area: 9,249 sq. mi.



## Virginia

Map on page 60
Population estimate: 6,768,400
Area: 39,597 sq. mi.



## Washington

Map on page 62
Population estimate: 5,674,900
Area: 66,582 sq. mi.



## West Virginia

Map on page 63
Population estimate: 1,813,200
Area: 24,087 sq. mi.



## Wisconsin

Map on page 64
Population estimate: 5,224,500
Area: 54,314 sq. mi.



## Wyoming

Map on page 65
Population estimate: 479,500
Area: 97,105 sq. mi.



## Canada

Map on page 66
Population estimate: 29,989,000
Area: 3,851,809 sq. mi.



## Mexico

Map on page 68
Population estimate: 102,912
Area: 761,606 sq. mi.



*Population estimates are for the year 2*